Listening &
Speaking Skills

Barry Cusack

Sam McCarter

MACMILLAN

Macmillan Education
Between Towns Road, Oxford OX4 3PP
A division of Macmillan Publishers Limited
Companies and representatives throughout the world

ISBN 978-0-230-00946-2

First published 2007

Original design by eMC Design; www.emcdesign.org.uk
Illustrated by eMC Design, Celia Hart
Cover design by Andrew Oliver
Cover photograph by Corbis/Tom Stewart

Barry Cusack would like to thank Nick Canham for his most valuable
advice and assistance.

The authors and publishers would like to thank the following for
permission to use copyright material: Adapted extract from
Open2.net website "The world around us" courtesy of the Open
University, reprinted by permission of the publisher.

The authors and publishers would like to thank the following for
permission to reproduce their photographic material:
Alamy/Janine Wiedel Photolibrary p30, Alamy/Stephen Bond
p46, Alamy/Photofusion Picture Library p54, Alamy/Alan Novelli
p62, Alamy/Chris Mole p70(m), Alamy/Mark A. Johnson p70(r),
Alamy/Chad Ehlers p78; **Corbis**/Carlos Dominguez p6(l), Corbis/Rolf
Bruderer p6(r), Corbis/Nation Wong/Zefa p23, Corbis/Royalty Free
p26; **Getty Images**/Harry Sheridan p70(l).

Printed in Thailand

2013 2012 2011 2010
11 10 9 8 7 6 5

Contents

Introduction
page 4

	Topic	Listening skills	Speaking skills
Unit 1 page 6	Change and consequences	Predicting in tables	Identifying yourself Discussing familiar topics Saying where you come from Pronunciation: word stress
Unit 2 page 14	The importance of the past	Signpost phrases Sentence completion Classification	Describing a past event Planning Describing precautions Pronunciation: *can* and *can't*
Unit 3 page 22	Machines, cycles, and processes	Information in flowcharts	Discussion questions Expressing views Pronunciation: emphasis
Unit 4 page 30	Education	Identifying campus contexts Information in multiple choice questions Summary completion	Describing people Making notes Pronunciation: stress shift
Unit 5 page 38	Youth	Understanding maps Sentence completion Table completion	Describing jobs Advantages and disadvantages Pronunciation: compound adjectives
Unit 6 page 46	Culture	Understanding layout Predicting from notes	Free time activities Expressing preferences Dealing with unfamiliar topics Pronunciation: *like* and *'d like*
Unit 7 page 54	Arts and sciences	Questions from statements Paraphrases for matching	Comparing and evaluating Expressing others' views Pronunciation: weak forms
Unit 8 page 62	Nature	Changing opinions Extended multiple choice Summary completion (2)	Describing animals Describing presents Making notes
Unit 9 page 70	Health	Predicting in tables (2) Words spelt out	Recognizing similar questions Emphasizing main points Taking time to think Pronunciation: contrastive stress
Unit 10 page 78	Individual and society	Paraphrasing questions Visual multiple choice	Places and feelings Starting your description Summing up impressions Pronunciation: past simple endings

Key and tapescripts
page 86

Introduction

What is *Improve your IELTS Listening and Speaking Skills*?

Improve your IELTS Listening and Speaking Skills is a complete preparation course for the Listening and Speaking Modules of the International English Language Testing System. Through targeted practice, it develops skills and language to help you achieve a higher IELTS score in these two modules.

How can I use this book?

You can use *Improve your IELTS Listening and Speaking Skills* as a book for studying on your own or in a class.

If you are studying on your own, *Improve Your IELTS Listening and Speaking Skills* is designed to guide you step-by-step through the activities. The book is completely self-contained: a clear and accessible key is provided, so you can easily check your answers as you work through the book. There are two CDs which contain all the recorded material necessary for the Listening skills and Speaking skills sections of each unit. There is also an audioscript which contains all the exam listening material on the CDs.

If you are studying as part of a class, your teacher will direct you on how to use each activity. Some activities, especially in the Topic talk and Speaking skills sections, provide the opportunity for speaking and discussion practice.

How is *Improve your IELTS Listening and Speaking Skills* organized?

It consists of ten units based around topics which occur commonly in the real test. Each unit consists of four sections:

Topic talk: exercises and activities to introduce vocabulary and ideas useful for the topic.

Listening skills: exercises and activities to develop the skills for questions in the Listening Module.

Speaking skills: exercises and activities to develop skills and language for the Speaking Module, including practice questions from one part of the Module.

Exam listening: one complete section of the Listening Module to practise the skills learned.

In addition, there are *Techniques* boxes throughout the book. These reinforce key points on how to approach Listening and Speaking tasks.

How will *Improve your IELTS Listening and Speaking Skills* improve my score?

By developing skills

The skills sections of each unit form a detailed syllabus of essential IELTS Listening and Speaking skills. For example, in Listening skills there is coverage of *Signpost phrases* and *Prediction skills*. In Speaking skills, there is coverage of *Comparing and evaluating* as well as *Describing advantages and disadvantages*. There is also Pronunciation practice at the end of the Speaking skills sections.

By developing language

The *Topic talk* part of each unit develops vocabulary, phrases, and sentence forms for use in the Listening and Speaking Modules. The Speaking skills section has phrases to help you introduce and organize your spoken answers.

By developing test technique

The Listening skills sections introduce you to the skills you need to tackle the various types of question that can be asked. Knowing the best way to tackle each type of question will enable you to get the best mark you can. The Speaking skills section will make you familiar with the different question-types and enable you to relax in the exam and perform at your best.

How is the IELTS Listening Module organized?

The Module consists of four sections: usually there are two monologues and two conversations on a variety of topics. There are ten questions in each section. The topics cover everyday social matters and subjects related to educational or training situations. You hear the recording only once, but you have time to look at the questions first and further time to write your answers.

What kind of questions are there?

The questions are of eight types: multiple choice, short answer questions, sentence completion, table completion, labelling a diagram, classification of information, matching information, and summary.

How will I be assessed?

You will get one mark for each correct answer up to a maximum of 40 marks. The questions get gradually harder, but all the marks have the same value.

How is the IELTS Speaking Module organized?

You have a one-to-one interview with an examiner lasting between eleven and fourteen minutes. There are three parts. First, the examiner asks questions on everyday topics such as family, hobbies, and likes and dislikes. Second, you speak for one to two minutes on a topic given by the examiner. Finally, you take part in a discussion on more abstract issues linked to the topic of the talk.

How will I be assessed?

The examiner awards marks under four headings:

Fluency and coherence: speaking in a continuous way, without unnatural hesitation, and organizing your thoughts and speech in a logical way.

Lexical resource: using a range of vocabulary appropriate to the topic.

Grammatical range and accuracy: using a range of grammatical forms, including more complex forms, with a reasonable degree of accuracy.

Pronunciation: speaking so that you can be understood by the examiner.

Change and Consequences

Unit aims

Listening skills

Predicting in tables

Speaking skills

Identifying yourself
Discussing familiar topics
Saying where you come from
Pronunciation: word stress

Topic talk

1 Look at the advertisements and answer the questions below.

Room available in large, central apartment in return for looking after pets and general duties. Must be reliable, tidy, and a non-smoker. Would suit female student.

Studio available. £400 a month, excluding bills. Twenty minutes by train from city. Single occupant only.

a Is rented accommodation expensive where you live? Why?
b How can students be helped with accommodation when they move away from home?
c Which accommodation above would you apply for? Why?

2 Complete sentences a–g with the words in the list.

Example

Here in Australia, I live in a ....flat....... in a twenty-storey tower block.

shared house   studio   farmhouse   house   flat   bungalow
penthouse   terraced house

a I'd love to live in a .... on the top floor of a tower block.
b In my home country, I live in the capital in a spacious detached ....
c I can't afford to live in a large flat so I am renting a small ....
d My parents live in a remote two-storey .... on a mountainside.
e As my grandmother can't climb stairs and hates lifts, she lives in a .... in the suburbs.
f My host family live in a red-brick .... right in the middle of a long row.
g There are six of us living together in a .... in a student area of town.

3 Add extra information to four of the sentences in 2 using phrases 1–4 below.

1 with spectacular views of the city, especially at night.
2 with lots of open fields around them and plenty of fresh air.
3 which has a kitchen, bedroom, living room all in one. It suits me fine.
4 which can get a bit noisy if all our friends are around.

4 Decide which adjective in a–g below is the opposite of the other two.

a boring dull fascinating
b cramped spacious sizeable
c traditional modern old-fashioned
d bustling quiet peaceful
e cosy uncomfortable inviting
f smart elegant shabby
g vibrant boring lively

5 Which type of accommodation do you live in? Make a list of adjectives to describe where you live.

6 The questions below come from an IELTS Speaking test. Match the examiner's questions with the candidate's answers.

1 Where do your host family live?
2 How close to the city is it?
3 Is your accommodation modern or old-fashioned?
4 Can you tell me what the area you live in is like?
5 What is your family home like?

a The neighbourhood where I live is very peaceful.
b My parents' apartment is in a very dynamic part of the city,
c The family I'm staying with live in a very chic part of town.
d The house is very high-tech,
e It is very well located,

7 Develop the sentences a–e in 6 by adding a phrase or sentence 1–5 below.

1 because it is well connected to the city centre by train and bus.
2 so it is always noisy and full of people.
3 with plasma screens, remote controls for the lighting, and wireless computers.
4 The area is residential with tree-lined streets, no shops and not many cars.
5 At all times of the day it is really tranquil. I have to say I love it there.

8 Which items in 7 give these extra types of information?

Reason ....
Consequence ....

9 With a partner, ask and answer the questions in 6.

1   Choose the best title a–c for each table 1–3.

   a   Climate change over 50 years
   b   Transport use by type
   c   Comparison of housing by area

1

District	Typical style	Average price	Transport
Aberton	bungalows	£180,000	1 ....
Hunborough	2	£225,000	poor
Millview	flats	3	excellent

2

	1955	2005
Average temperature	17.4°	4 ....
Annual rainfall	5	652 mm

3

	Bus	Train	Bicycle
Price of fare	£1.50	7	N/A
Total journeys	6	2504	962
Male passengers	34%	62%	8 ....
Female	66%	38%	9 ....

2   Complete each table with the information below.

£125,000   £2.20   18.2°   25%   3,567   612 mm   75%
good   terraced houses

3   Look at the numbering in the tables. Which tables are read from top to bottom? Which are read from left to right?

4 The table below is taken from a table completion task. Read the table contents and then answer questions a–d. Write NO MORE THAN TWO WORDS AND/OR A NUMBER for each answer.

	Price now	**Main advantage**	**Second advantage**	**Length of guarantee**	**Main disadvantage**
Analogue radio	Example: £29.99	Cheap	Excellent **3** .... with expensive systems	**4**	Service will finish at some time
Digital radio	**1** £	**2** Lots of	Little or no interference	2 years	**5** .... is short

a What is the topic of the table?
b How many products are discussed?
c How many aspects of each product are considered?
d Which answers may be numbers?

Technique

In table completion tasks, pay special attention to the rubric, the headings, and the numbering. Use this information to predict the type of information which is missing.

5 Look again at the instructions for the table completion task in 4. Which of these answers must be wrong?

a very high quality   c £35 or £55
b 210   d 3 or 4 years

6 1.1 Listen to the recording, follow the instructions and complete the gaps in the table.

7 The table below is also taken from a table completion task. Read through the table carefully and answer these questions.

a In which order will you hear the information?
b Which answers can you predict?

	old ValueCard	**new SuperValue Card**
Points	Standard number	Double points
Free credit period	One month	**6** .... months
Interest rate	18.5%	**7** .... %
Cardholder shopping evenings	**8** .... per month	Two per month
Benefits	Free delivery within **9** .... miles	Free delivery within 50 miles
Fee	Nil	**10** £ ....

8 1.2 Listen to the recording and complete the gaps in the table. Write NO MORE THAN TWO WORDS AND/OR A NUMBER for each answer.

1   🔊 1.3 Listen to four questions from the start of the IELTS Speaking test. Write the exact questions the examiner asks.

a   Can you …
b   And what …
c   Where …
d   Could you …

2   Read this information about a candidate for the Speaking test. Use the information to complete the dialogue with the examiner.

> Benjamin Weiss is going to take the Speaking Module at 3.30 this afternoon. He comes from Switzerland and prefers people to call him Ben. He has brought his passport as identification.

Candidate: Hello, good ………………… .

Examiner: Good ………………… . Can you ………………… me your …………………

name, please?

Candidate: My name is ………………… .

Examiner: And what can I ………………… you?

Candidate: Please ………………… me ………………… .

Examiner: Good. Where ………………… you come ………………… ?

Candidate: I come ………………… .

Examiner: Can you ………………… me your identification, please?

Candidate: Of course. ………………… is my ………………… .

3   With a partner, practise reading the dialogue in 2. Then practise again giving answers as yourself.

Discussing familiar topics

4   The following questions are taken from an interview in a daily newspaper with a famous singer. Match the questions 1–8 with her answers a–h.

1   What kind of town did you grow up in?

2   Where would you like to live?

3   Do you have any hobbies?

4   What sort of TV programmes do you like watching?

5   What is your greatest fear?

6   Which living person do you most admire?

7   What is your most precious object?

8   What sort of place do you live in now?

a I've got this beautiful ring that belonged to my grandmother. It has sentimental value for me. It's very special.

b Spiders.

c In New York, of course.

d I'm quite keen on comedies. I don't particularly like news and current affairs. It makes me feel sad.

e Hotels mostly.

f I grew up in quite a small town. It was quiet and nice, and everyone seemed to know everyone else.

g I like playing jazz piano. I like it because it relaxes me.

h My dad. He has taught me such a lot about how to live my life well, and I'm grateful for that.

5 Look again at the questions and answers in 4. Answer the questions below.

a Are the questions complex and abstract or do they relate to personal information?

b Which answers would be good in the Speaking test? Why?

Technique

It is useful to prepare for Speaking Part 1 by thinking of the kinds of topics you are likely to be asked about. Prepare by thinking of extra details to support your answers.

6 Write at least two simple questions about each of the topics below.

Example

What types of music do you like listening to?

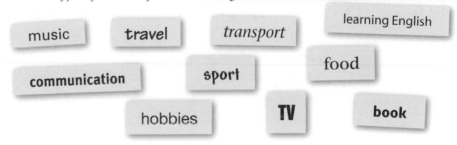

music   travel   transport   learning English

communication   sport   food

hobbies   TV   book

7 With a partner, ask and answer the questions you wrote in 6. Give extra information to elaborate your answers.

Saying where you come from

8 1.4 In Speaking Part 1, you will often be asked about your home town or where you live now. Listen to an extract from an interview. Complete the examiner's questions in the spaces below.

Now in this first part I'd like to ask you some questions about yourself. Let's talk about your town or village.

Question 1:	Could you tell me …
Question 2:	What …
Question 3:	Is there anything …
Question 4:	And what kind …

9 1.4 Listen again. Make notes on the details that the student mentions in response to each question. How much detail does the student give?

Question 1 ....

Question 2 ....

Question 3 ....

Question 4 ....

10 Make a note of your own personal answers in response to the questions in 8.

11 With a partner, ask and answer the questions in 8. Try to add more details to elaborate your answers. Use the phrases in the list below to help you.

I used to live in … but now I …

I moved here …

It's a … place with …

What I like about it is … because …

The great thing about … is …

I suppose most people …

> **Technique**
>
> Always elaborate your answers using extra details.

Pronunciation: word stress

12 How many syllables are there in each of these words for describing places?

> pleasant   dynamic   flat   peaceful   cramped   bungalow
> detached   overpriced

13 1.5 Listen to the words and match each word with a stress pattern below.

Example

pleasant   *pattern 2*

Pattern 1 O
Pattern 2 Oo
Pattern 3 oO
Pattern 4 Ooo
Pattern 5 oOo
Pattern 6 ooO

14 Identify which word does not belong to each set of words below.

a	pretend	also	although	repair
b	interest	social	special	offend
c	quality	radio	example	comedy
d	exactly	expensive	advantage	certainly
e	depend	remote	open	create
f	unpleasant	fabulous	specialize	operate
g	intend	cancel	prefer	reply

Exam listening

Section 2

 1.6

Questions 11–15

Write **NO MORE THAN THREE WORDS AND/OR A NUMBER** *for each answer.*

What three kinds of people are listening to the talk?

11 ....

12 ....

13 ....

14 What will you need to do to visit the Fieldhouse Library?

....

15 What is necessary for gaining access to the library?

....

1.7

Questions 16–20

Write **NO MORE THAN TWO WORDS AND/OR A NUMBER** *for each answer.*

What are the two collections which have not yet been fully moved in?

16 ....

17 ....

18 What is currently being built?

....

19 How many computer places have been installed?

....

20 What else can you get from the librarians if you ask?

....

The importance of the past

Unit aims

Listening skills	Speaking skills
Signpost phrases	Describing a past event
Sentence completion	Planning
Classification	Describing precautions
	Pronunciation: *can* and *can't*

Topic talk

1 Look at the pictures and answer the questions which follow.

    a   What do you think each item reminds the speaker of?
    b   Does the train ticket trigger happy or sad memories? How do you know?
    c   Is there anything which triggers happy memories for you? If so, what?

2 In the IELTS Speaking test, you can be asked to describe events from your personal history. In the phrases below, decide which two adjectives are connected with positive memory.

Example

good unforgettable ceremonial moment

    a   suitable marvellous great time
    b   happy tragic remarkable event
    c   great momentous formal occasion
    d   fleeting memorable favourable moment
    e   exhilarating rewarding past experience
    f   exciting big foreign adventure
    g   outstanding minor impressive achievement
    h   former golden happy days
    i   fantastic business great trip

3 Which words from the lists in 2 combine with the words below? Complete the lists. The first one has been done for you.

thoroughly *exciting*, …
highly …
very …
totally …

4 Match each event a–e with the noun which best describes it.

an achievement
an adventure
an event
a special occasion
an experience

a studying abroad
b doing well in exams
c a musical concert
d your brother's wedding
e getting lost

5 In the IELTS Speaking test, use nouns like those in 4 to help trigger ideas. For each noun in the list, think of at least one personal experience.

Example

an achievement: *I won a school sports prize.*

6 With a partner, ask and answer questions about the events you noted in 5. Use these prompts to help you.

Tell me about …
What kind of …?
What happened …?

7 In the IELTS Speaking test, use nouns to summarize descriptions. Match each event a–h with the descriptions below.

Example

I had a party for my twenty-first birthday. *It was a happy event.*

a I volunteered to help other young people.
b I received first prize for a painting when I was in secondary school.
c I want to describe something strange which actually happened in my home town.
d The journey by coach and train around South America brings back lots of good memories.
e I attended the inaugural speech of the President.
f I got lost with some friends in the Australian desert.
g I parachuted from a plane to celebrate passing my exams.
h I saw the hardship of other people when I was volunteering.

exhilarating experience
unforgettable moment
formal occasion
rewarding experience
nerve-racking adventure
bizarre incident
humbling experience
memorable trip

1   The sentences below come from a lecture on history. Decide the function of the phrases in italic in sentences a–i and add them to the lists. The first one has been done for you.

Starting: *e*, …
Listing: …
Adding: …
Digressing: …
Returning to the subject …
Concluding: …

a   *In addition*, we can ask if the study of history has any practical use.
b   *Anyway*, there is a wide range of topics for you to choose from.
c   *Finally*, I wish you good luck.
d   *By the way*, there is a series of lectures on this topic starting on Tuesday.
e   *I'd like to begin* this term's lectures *with* a few general questions.
f   *Secondly*, what is history?
g   *To sum up*, as I said, you are fortunate.
h   *Firstly*, why study history?
i   *Again*, we can look at the different kinds of history there are to study.

2   The sentences below are part of another lecture on a similar topic. Put them in the correct order.

a   By the way, there's a lecture on citizenship in the Social Sciences building on Tuesday.
b   I'd like to begin by giving three reasons for studying history.
c   Finally, we can do better in our jobs if we know a little history.
d   Secondly, it helps us to be better citizens: we can participate better in our society if we understand its history.
e   Firstly, it helps us to understand the world we live in, especially its politics and economics.
f   To sum up, history can be a huge help for many aspects of our lives.
g   Anyway, our participation in society is more meaningful if we understand a bit more.

Sentence completion

3   Statements a–f give some facts about sentence completion tasks. Decide whether the statements are true or false.

a   You must always put words in the gaps.
b   The instructions tell you how many words you need.
c   Sometimes you can put a number in the gap.
d   The missing information is usually at the start of the sentence.
e   Gaps are located at the middle or end of the sentence.
f   It is possible to guess what type of information is missing.

Technique

Talks and lectures are frequently organized using predictable linking phrases. Pay attention to these. They will help you to follow the flow and structure of the recording in Listening Section 4.

4 The instructions and sentences below are taken from a sentence completion task. Read them carefully and check your answers to 3.

*Complete the sentences below. Write **NO MORE THAN ONE WORD AND/OR A NUMBER** for each answer.*

The handout covers **1** .... general topics.

As well as students of history, there are students of **2** .... at the lecture.

The lecturer's own motivation for studying history is that she finds it **3** ....

5 1.8 Listen to the first part of the recording and answer the questions in 4.

Classification

6 The inventions in the list come from different periods in history. Decide which period A–C they belong to.

A	the eighteenth century	1	the telephone
B	the nineteenth century	2	the automobile
C	the twentieth century	3	the steam engine
		4	the aeroplane
		5	the typewriter
		6	the wristwatch

7 Imagine you are listening to a lecture on the inventions in 6. What information would help you classify the inventions?

8 The questions below are taken from a classification task. Can you predict any of the answers? What words or expressions do you expect to hear?

How does the lecturer describe each kind of history?

T   a traditional type of history
M   a modern type of history
F   a type of history which looks to the future

Write the correct letter T, M, or F next to questions 4–10.

4	political history	....
5	post-modern history	....
6	feminist history	....
7	social history	....
8	economic history	....
9	military history	....
10	ethnic history	....

Technique

In classification tasks, read the question carefully. If the categories are related, decide what kinds of words and phrases you would expect to hear. Listen for similar information in the recording.

9 1.9 Listen to the second part and classify the types of history in 8.

1   Read these two advertisements and answer questions a–d.

   a   Where would you see advertisements like these?
   b   Do you think the owner will find her purse? What about the owner of the wallet?
   c   What do you think about the reward? Is it large enough, or too large?
   d   What would you do if you lost a wallet or a purse?

> ## FOUND
> Lady's purse.
> Cards, keys and other things inside.
> First person to describe the contents accurately will have it.
> Ask inside shop.

> **LOST**
> I have lost my wallet with £30 in cash and credit card inside.
> Also photo of cat. Reward: £10.
> Phone: **07956 23498**

2   Read the list of personal objects below. Number each object 1–10 according to how inconvenient it would be to lose (1 = most inconvenient; 10 = least inconvenient).

house keys	folding umbrella	theatre tickets	£100 in cash
diary	student card	£5 in cash	hotel room key
	mobile phone	credit card	

3   1.10 Listen to a man telling a story about an object he lost. What did he lose? How important was it?

4   1.10 Listen again and match each phrase a–d from the story with the correct function 1–4.

   a   I should say
   b   How shall I put it?
   c   Now, where was I?
   d   Let me see,

   1   returning to the subject
   2   filling in
   3   emphasizing a point
   4   searching for a word

Planning

5   The taskcard below is taken from Speaking Part 2. Read the card and answer question a–c below.

Describe an important thing that you lost and what happened when you lost it.

You should say

    why the thing was important to you

    how you lost it

    what efforts you made to find it

and explain what you will do in future.

---

a   What is the main topic?
b   How many separate instructions are there?
c   How many instructions relate to the future? How many relate to the past?

6   The notes below were made by a student who was preparing to give a talk on the card above. Which instructions on the card does each note relate to?

> 1   ⟶ shop
> 2   ⟶ police
> 3   bag with shoulder strap
> 4   handbag
> 5   cards!
> 6   ⟶ newspaper
> 7   ? shop

> **Technique**
>
> You have only one minute to think and make notes for your talk. The maximum you have time to write is about ten words. Use the notes to help start you off, then talk around them.

7   Imagine you are the student who wrote the notes in 6. Practise giving a short talk using the notes. Use some of the phrases below to help you.

Well, I should say first that
To find it, I first
After that, I
Finally, I
Looking back, I realize that
In future I will (not)

8   Take one minute to think and make notes about your own talk on this topic, using your own experience. Then practise speaking for two minutes using your notes.

Describing precautions

9 Read the example sentence below. Underline the phrase which indicates that it is a precaution.

Example

In future, I will put labels on my suitcases in case they get lost on the plane.

10 Match each precaution a–f below with a situation 1–6 that it might prevent. Rewrite the sentences using the structure in 9.

    a   Put some keys in a flower pot in the front garden.
    b   Keep a note of your password.
    c   Note the phone number of your embassy in the country you are visiting.
    d   Keep a second umbrella in the car.
    e   Keep a twenty pound note in your shoe.
    f   Write down the phone number of your bank.

    1   You leave yours at home.
    2   You lose your passport.
    3   Somebody robs you in the street.
    4   You lose your credit card.
    5   You lose your house keys.
    6   You can't get into your emails.

11 The taskcard below is taken from Speaking Part 2. Take a minute to think and make notes. Then practise speaking for two minutes.

Describe a time when you were late for an event.

You should say

    what kind of event you were late for

    what caused you to arrive late

    what happened to you when you arrived

and explain what you have learned from the experience.

Pronunciation: *can* and *can't*

12 1.11 Listen and complete sentences a–d with the correct word *can* or *can't*.

    a   I .... remember my favourite childhood toy.
    b   I .... remember my first holiday.
    c   I .... recall a time when I got lost.
    d   My first day at school was a day I .... forget.

13 Practise saying aloud the sentences in 12.

14 For each memory below, say what you *can* and *can't* remember about it.

> your first home   your favourite toy   your best friend
> your first day at school   a park   playing sports
> going on your first holiday   getting lost

Exam listening

Section 3

 1.12

Questions 21–25

*Complete the sentences below. Write **NO MORE THAN THREE WORDS AND/OR A NUMBER** for each answer.*

The name of the assignment is 'Museums – their **21** .... '.

The number one problem with local museums is that they are **22** ....

The purpose of the museum shop is to **23** ....

The boat was **24** .... years old.

The **25** .... are dark.

 1.13

Questions 26–30

How does Tom think the museums should be funded?

A   *by the state*
B   *by local government*
C   *by private funding*

*Write the correct letter **A**, **B**, or **C** next to Questions 26–30.*

26   local history museums   ....

27   natural history museums   ....

28   science museums   ....

29   craft museums   ....

30   working farms   ....

Machines, processes, and cycles

Unit aims

Listening skills

Information in flowcharts

Speaking skills

Discussion questions
Expressing views
Pronunciation: emphasis

Topic talk

1 Read the dialogue and answer the questions a–d.

Customer I bought this camera from you over the Internet and when it arrived it was damaged.

Call Centre Oh dear, I'm sorry about that. What exactly was wrong with it?

Customer: Well first of all, …

a Is it safe to shop over the Internet?
b What do you think the main effects of Internet shopping are?
c Have you bought anything over the Internet? If not, would you?
d Have you ever bought anything which was damaged? What did you do?

2 From the following four options, which three problems do you think the customer listed?

a The lens is scratched.
b There's something wrong with the lid.
c The lens cover is missing.
d The zoom lens doesn't work.

3 Which of the materials below can be categorized as cloth and which as metal? Which are man-made?

fur gold cotton wood linen polyester aluminium silk
brass glass plastic tin leather steel

4 Name a common object which you would use the words below to describe.

Example

spherical: *football*

spherical rectangular square circular oval spiral

5 In the IELTS Speaking test, you may have to describe an object. Describe in your own words an object that you have bought, without saying its name. Ask another student to guess the object.

6 In Listening Section 1, you may hear a conversation between a customer and a shop assistant. Match the complaints about the objects in 1–8 with the product details a–h.

1 I bought this software CD and it won't work.
2 There is something wrong with the frame of my sunglasses.
3 I can't get the new TV to work properly.
4 I'm ringing to complain about the vase you sent.
5 The box had a sticker with 'handle with care' on it, but it was torn.
6 The PC monitor won't switch on.
7 I washed this jumper.
8 The book got here on time, but it was damaged.

a And when I looked inside the contents were crushed and broken.
b The arms are too tight.
c When it arrived, the cover was ripped.
d I think the connection is loose.
e The picture only appears in black and white.
f When it arrived, it had completely shattered.
g I get an error message, and it just keeps jamming in the machine.
h And it has just fallen apart.

7 Complete the table below with a possible fault from the list. You may use each word only once.

| wobbly ripped uncomfortable snapped jammed cracked |
| scratched twisted faded leaking |

Object	Component	Fault
a trousers	leg	....
b food blender	bowl	....
c backpack	zip	....
d jumper	colour	....
e mirror	glass	....
f sandals	strap	....
g CD	surface	....
h bicycle	seat	....
i memory stick	prong	....
j table	leg	....

8 Make sentences using ideas from 7. Use the sentences below and add appropriate adverbs from the list.

| very badly severely completely slightly |

You sent me this/these .... and I was really annoyed to find that ...

When I opened the .... you sent, I found the ...

1 The flowchart below is used by a mail order company to indicate how customer queries should be dealt with. Match notes a–d with the correct spaces in the flowchart.

    a   Ask purpose of customer's call
    b   Request to place order
    c   Put customer on hold
    d   Can query be dealt with over telephone?

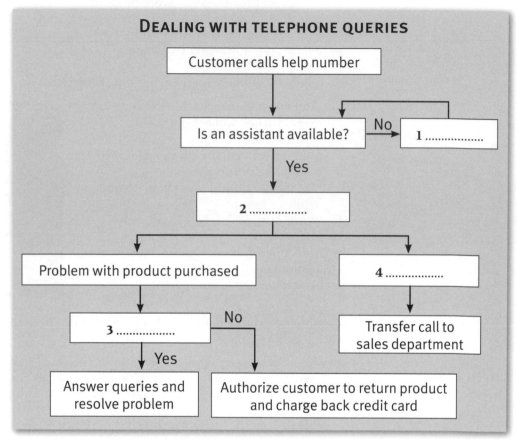

DEALING WITH TELEPHONE QUERIES

Customer calls help number

Is an assistant available? — No → 1 ....

Yes

2 ....

Problem with product purchased

3 .... — No

Yes

Answer queries and resolve problem

Authorize customer to return product and charge back credit card

4 ....

Transfer call to sales department

2 A flowchart in an IELTS Listening task indicates that information is related in particular ways. Label each phrase in the box with the relationship it indicates. Choose from: *cause and effect, conditional,* or *linear ordering.*

> As a result   This means that   If ... , then   Firstly   Otherwise   Next
> Unless ... , then   This leads to   Finally   If not, then   To begin with

3 Imagine that a training manager is describing the procedure above for dealing with customer queries. Which phrases from 2 would you expect to hear? Write the phrases on the flowchart in the appropriate places.

4 The information opposite is taken from a flowchart task. Answer questions a–d.

    a   What is the starting point and end point of the process?
    b   What is the general topic?
    c   Which nouns and verbs appear many times in the chart?
    d   Which words from 2 above do you expect to hear and where?

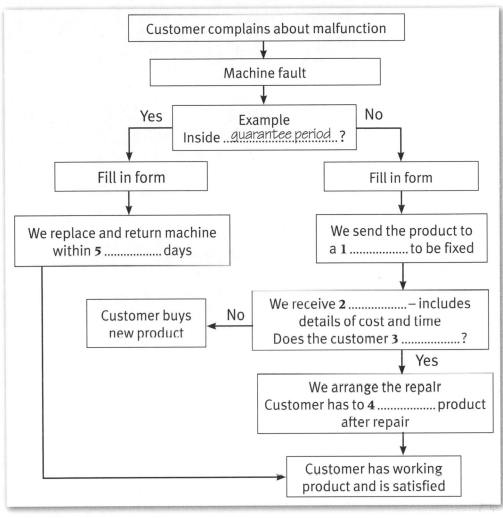

5 1.14 Listen to the first part of the recording and complete the gaps in the flowchart. Write NO MORE THAN TWO WORDS AND/OR A NUMBER for each answer.

6 1.15 The form below is taken from a form completion task, which follows on from the flowchart in 5. Listen to the recording and complete the form. Write NO MORE THAN ONE WORD AND/OR A NUMBER for each answer.

Harvey's Homewares
Faulty Product Replacement Instruction
Product Make: Gleeware
Model: Breadmaker 3
Model No: **6** ....
Shop where bought: Bluewater
Date of purchase: 2.12.06.
Customer surname: **7** .... Initials: J.H
House number: **8** ....   Road name: **9** .... Gardens
Postcode: AD22 4SC
Home phone: 08896 3412877
Day of delivery: **10** ....

1 There are many influences on the way people shop. Number each factor below 1–8 according to how much you think it influences what you buy (1 = most important; 8 = least important).

> advertising   convenience   fashion   luxury   necessity   quality
> shop service   value for money

2 For each of the factors you rated 1–3 above, think of a purchase you made where that factor influenced you. Tell another student about this experience.

3 Statements a–h below relate to the topic of shopping. Decide which of the statements you agree and disagree with.

   a   Shopping habits have been changed by globalization.
   b   Shopping can be a form of relaxation.
   c   The Internet will eventually mean the end of shopping as we know it.
   d   People worldwide are becoming more materialistic.
   e   Shopping today is a less personal process than shopping in the past.
   f   The purpose of advertising is to inform people about what is available.
   g   Discarded packaging is causing serious environmental problems.
   h   Shopping in local markets is preferable to shopping in big stores.

4 Speaking Part 3 discussion questions are often formed in predictable ways. Read the examples below. Then invent similar questions based on the statements above using the question prompts given.

Examples

   a   *In what ways* have shopping habits been changed by globalization?
   b   *To what extent is* shopping a form of relaxation?

To what extent
In what ways
What are the main differences between
What
Which do you prefer:
How

5   1.16 Listen to three people answering questions on the topics in 1. Identify which topic they are discussing and write the question they are answering in the spaces below.

Speaker 1: ....

Speaker 2: ....

Speaker 3: ....

Expressing views

6   1.16 Listen again. For each speaker, make a note of the phrases they use to introduce their opinions.

Speaker 1: ....

Speaker 2: ....

Speaker 3: ....

Technique

In Speaking Part 3, you are expected to discuss some questions related to a topic. Use phrases which show that you able to communicate your own ideas effectively.

7   With a partner, ask and answer the questions you wrote in 4. Use the phrases for expressing views below to state your own opinions.

Phrase bank
In my view/opinion,
Well, from my point of view,
To my mind,
It seems to me that
Personally, I think
My impression is that
I suppose

8   Read the three short texts about fashion. To what extent do you agree with the ideas expressed?

The fashion cycle

As everyone knows, what's in fashion today was probably in fashion twenty years ago. However, cheap imported clothes have meant that the fashion cycle is getting shorter and shorter. Whereas in the past people made their clothes last longer, people today replace their wardrobe more regularly, encouraged by the media and advertisers.

You are what you wear

A generation ago, what teenagers wore to school was not a matter of choice. They had to wear a uniform. To some extent, the same was true of adults who wore serious business suits in the office. Nowadays, things are rather different: schoolchildren can customize their uniform; adults have dress-down days. With this has come more anxiety about looking good and creating the right impression.

Keeping up with the Joneses

When people talk about fashion, they often have clothes in mind, but, in a way, fashion affects all aspects of our lives. People spend money on redecorating their houses, on eating organic food, or on the latest four-wheel-drive car because they perceive these things to be fashionable, not because they need them. That's not a criticism, it's just human nature.

9 Match each text with one of the Speaking Part 3 questions a–c below.

   a   In what ways does fashion affect different aspects of our lives?
   b   What makes people follow fashion?
   c   To what extent does how we dress indicate who we are?

10 With another student, ask and answer the questions in 9. Give your own views.

Pronunciation: emphasis

11 Read these opinions about advertising. Underline the main stress in the phrases in italic.

   a   *In my view,* there is too much advertising on television.
   b   *To my mind,* advertising is fun.
   c   *It seems to me* that advertising does more harm than good.
   d   *My impression is* that most advertising is misleading.

12 1.17 Listen to the recording and review your answer. Which word carries the main stress in the phrases?

13 Give your opinion on these statements, using the phrases above.

   a   Internet shopping is a great thing.
   b   Fashions change too quickly.
   c   Excessive packaging of products like groceries should be prohibited.
   d   Shopping is hard work.

Exam listening

Section 4

 1.18

Questions 31–35

Complete the sentences below.

Write **NO MORE THAN TWO WORDS OR A NUMBER** *for each answer.*

Recycling is principally the responsibility of **31** ....

The second stage in the cycle relates to acquiring **32** .... in general.

Harvesting includes cutting down trees and **33** ....

Chemical processes create **34** ....

A significant proportion of the **35** .... stage is unnecessary.

Questions 36–40

Complete the flowchart.

Write **NO MORE THAN TWO WORDS OR A NUMBER** *for each answer*

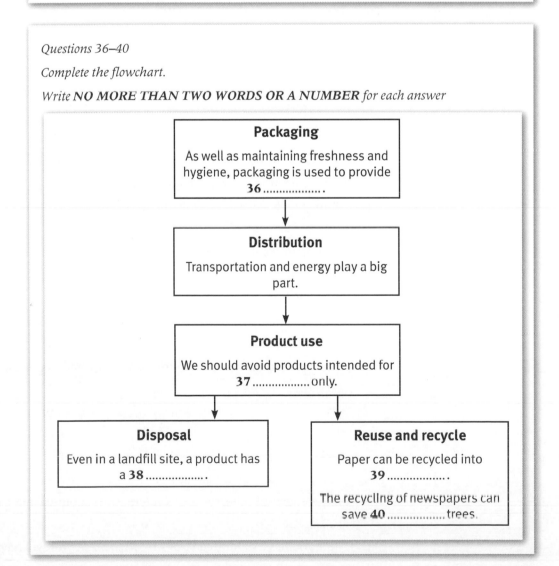

Packaging

As well as maintaining freshness and hygiene, packaging is used to provide **36** ....

↓

Distribution

Transportation and energy play a big part.

↓

Product use

We should avoid products intended for **37** .... only.

Disposal

Even in a landfill site, a product has a **38** ....

Reuse and recycle

Paper can be recycled into **39** ....

The recycling of newspapers can save **40** .... trees.

Education

Topic talk

1 Look at the photo and answer the questions below.

a   Would you describe the situation in the photo as a tutorial, a seminar, or a lecture? What is the difference?

b   Which of the three modes of teaching do you think is the best way of learning?

c   What are the differences or similarities between teaching in universities in your home country and other parts of the world like the UK?

2   Listening Section 3 often relates to academic courses. Complete the sentences below about courses with nouns from the list.

> requirements   analysis   criteria   dissertation   essay   evaluation
> module   paper   portfolio   programme

a   In order to study photography, you have to fulfil the *course* .... , which include a foundation qualification in art.

b   Many people fail at medicine due to the difficulty of meeting the *assessment* ....

c   Most mature students enrol on a *part-time* ....

d   At the start of each academic year, students choose which *core* .... they will take.

e   As part of their jobs, many lecturers are expected to submit at least one *academic* .... per year.

f   Students on the fine art programme are required to present a .... *of their work*.

g   After collecting your data, you will need to carry out an *in-depth* .... of it.

h   To get a good mark, students should show they are capable of making a *critical* .... of the literature.

i   At the end of the course, each student must submit a 4,000-word *long* ....

j   After you have submitted your MA .... , you will have to wait about four months for your final grade.

3 Look at the sentences in 2 again. Which verb introduces the noun in each case?

4 The steps below give details of how to prepare a piece of written work as part of a course. Work with another student. Put the stages a–g in a logical order.

a present an analysis of the data
b include a bibliography
c describe the methods used for collecting data
d set out your hypothesis and explain your terms of reference
e draw conclusions based on your analysis
f provide a survey of existing literature
g state your aims and objectives

5 The statements a–j below were made by students about courses they are taking. Complete each sentence with a feature from the list.

> research project   deadlines   easy-going tutors
> end-of-year examination   background reading list   extensions
> weekly seminars   individual tuition   ongoing assessment
> practical work   vocational content

a The tutors provide you with a .... before the course.

b As part of our assessment, we have to plan and carry out a ....

c It's a very flexible programme: we have very ....

d It can get very stressful: we are assessed by ....

e Coursework has really fixed .... You can't get ....

f Everyone gets .... if they are experiencing difficulties.

g The course is marked by .... of written work.

h I spend a lot of time doing .... in a laboratory.

i It's mostly .... : it will all be useful for my career.

j There are regular .... in which people take turns to make presentations.

6 With a partner, discuss these questions about the statements in 5.

a Which statements would attract you to take a course? Which would put you off?
b Have you had experiences similar to these? If so, tell your partner about what happened to you.

1 Listening Section 3 is normally set in a place of academic study. Complete each list below with nouns that you normally associate with them. The first ones have been done for you.

a   library   *journals,*
b   student flat   *study bedroom,*
d   lecture theatre   *aisles,*
e   laboratory   *experiment,*

2 Look at multiple-choice questions 1 and 2 in 3 below. What words do you think might indicate the correct answer?

Information in multiple-choice questions

3 The questions below are taken from a multiple-choice task. The questions and options can give you a lot of information about what you will hear. Read multiple-choice questions 1–4 and answer questions a–d.

a   How many speakers do you think you will hear?
b   Who has to do assignments?
c   Which academic subjects is someone studying?
d   What area of that subject are they focusing on?

---

1   Where are the speakers having this discussion?

   A   a library

   B   a student flat

   C   a lecture theatre

2   How has Chloe spent the morning?

   A   drinking coffee

   B   training

   C   studying

3   According to Bill, what does the experiment show?

   A   Quantities of water are hard to measure.

   B   Children under five make many mistakes.

   C   Clear thinking is difficult for small children.

4   Bill's assignment is about the stages in a child's

   A   emotional development.

   B   mental development.

   C   social development.

---

4   1.19 Listen to the first part of this Listening Section 3 recording and answer Questions 1–4 above, choosing the correct answer A, B, or C.

Summary completion

5 The list below gives eight popular degree subjects. Number each subject 1–10 according to how easy or difficult you think each subject is (1 = easiest; 10 = most difficult).

> psychology   medicine   engineering   law   languages
> business management   physics   sports science   sociology   fine art

6 Compare your answers with another student. Then answer the questions below.

a   Which of these subjects would you prefer to study? Why?
b   How far would you agree that the most popular subjects also tend to be the easiest?
c   Which subjects have you enjoyed studying most in the past? Why?

7 The paragraph below is taken from a summary completion task.

a   Which speaker does it concentrate on?
b   What aspect of her studies does it discuss?

> Chloe started the psychology course in the **5** .... year. Previously she studied law. She enjoyed studying the **6** .... branch of that subject. The worst thing was having to remember lots of **7** .... She found **8** .... especially technical. She did not enjoy spending her time reading about **9** .... in the library. The part of the psychology course she likes best is experimental psychology, because it involves **10** .... activities.

Technique

Use the reading time to think about the overall topic of the summary. The general topic of each answer may be clear from the context.

8 Match each of the predictions below with a gap in the paragraph in 7. Think of any other predictions you can add.

a   It's an area of law, but it's technical, so maybe it's something like *property law*.
b   It's an area of law, and it's interesting, so maybe it's something like *family law*.
c   It's something that goes with activities, like *useful* or *difficult*.
d   This is something like *last*, or an ordinal number like *second*.
e   Something you have to remember, like *names* or *dates*.
f   It's something lawyers read about, like *judgements*.

9 🎧 1.20 Listen to the second recording and complete the summary. Write NO MORE THAN THREE WORDS for each answer.

Speaking skills   Describing people

1   Answer the questions below about the teachers you had at school.

   a   How well do you remember your teachers?

   b   Was there a teacher you especially liked? Why?

   c   How in general can teachers make lessons more interesting and fun? Is it important to do this? Is it always possible to do this?

2   The list below gives some qualities that teachers might possess. Decide if each quality is Important (I), Useful (U), or Not important (N).

Qualities of good teachers

They speak many foreign languages.   ....

They have a lot of hobbies.   ....

They set high standards.   ....

They are able to explain difficult things.   ....

They tell lots of jokes.   ....

They maintain discipline.   ....

They avoid negative criticism.   ....

They speak loudly.   ....

They give a lot of praise.   ....

They are very athletic.   ....

They mark and return students' work quickly.   ....

They are good-looking.   ....

They know the subject well.   ....

They are polite to the students.   ....

3   Which other qualities would you add to the list?

4   1.21 The taskcard below is taken from Speaking Part 2. Listen to a person answering the question. Make a brief note on the card of the answers they give to each prompt.

Describe a teacher you can remember from your schooldays.

You should say

   what this teacher looked like

   what subjects they taught

   what kind of person they were

and explain how this person has influenced you.

Technique

In Speaking Part 2, use phrases to structure your talk and help you move on to the next point.

5 Match each phrase in the list to one of the functions a–d.

a   Introducing your choice.
b   Explaining the reason for your choice.
c   Describing physical features.
d   Describing character.

Physically, he/she was …
The … I've chosen is …
What … taught me was that …
In terms of personality, …
I can remember … really well.
He/she looked …
Character-wise, he/she was …
I'll never forget him/her because …

6   1.21 Listen again. Which phrases from 5 does the speaker use?

7 Take one minute to think and make notes about your own talk on this topic, using your own experience. Then practise speaking for two minutes using your notes and the phrases in 5.

Making notes

8 Another student made the notes below for the Speaking Part 2 task in 4. Add the words in the list below to the appropriate part of the diagram.

short
fat
amusing
relaxed
looked out of the window while speaking
rolled tie up and down
made boring subjects interesting
made difficult subjects easy
cheerful personality

9 The notes in A and B below describe the advantages and disadvantages of different ways of making notes. Answer the questions below.

  a   Which list relates to the technique in 8?
  b   What kind of note-taking does the other list describe?
  c   Which method of making notes would work best for you?

List A
encourages creative thinking
many ways through the ideas
takes little time to write
uses very few words
can be messy

List B
encourages logical thinking
one way through the ideas
can take a long time to write
uses more words
very tidy

10 Using a note-taking technique you prefer, make notes on the Speaking Part 2 taskcard below, using your own experience. Then practise speaking for two minutes using your notes.

> Describe a person you know who has helped you in some way.
>
> You should say
>
> > how you know this person
> >
> > what abilities this person has
> >
> > how this person helped you
>
> and explain how this help has influenced your life.

Pronunciation: stress

11 Put the words in brackets in the right place in the sentences.

  a   Sarah has lots of .... and ideas. I can't .... our office without her. (imagine, imagination)

  b   Bill is able to .... other people and he has a high level of .... himself. (motivate, motivation)

  c   Jack has an .... outlook, whereas Tom is one of life's .... (pessimists, optimistic)

  d   Jack is an .... and deals with our publicity. But Tom is very .... , too. (artist, artistic)

12 1.22 Underline the stress on each word you have put in, eg i<u>ma</u>gine. Then listen to the recording to check.

13 Think of a group you work or study with and answer these questions.

  a   Who has the following things: *communication skills, motivation, imagination, good qualifications*?
  b   Who is: *artistic, optimistic, diplomatic*?

Exam listening

Section 4

 1.23

Questions 31–35

Choose the correct letter **A**, **B**, *or* **C**.

31 How long would terms be under the six-term system?

   A six weeks

   B seven weeks

   C thirteen weeks

32 What would happen to the summer holiday?

   A It would disappear.

   B It would be shortened.

   C It would be lengthened.

33 How much was the average learning loss in the summer?

   A two weeks

   B three weeks

   C seven weeks

34 In which subject was learning loss greatest among disadvantaged children?

   A maths

   B reading

   C writing

35 According to Marchmont's research, in the six-term system pupils performed

   A better than under the existing system.

   B worse than under the existing system.

   C the same as under the existing system.

Questions 36–40

Complete the summary below. Write **NO MORE THAN TWO WORDS** *for each answer.*

The school terms that we use originated when many people worked in **36** .... Also, because of the heat, it was difficult to teach children in July and August before the invention of **37** .... A different approach can be provided by the **38** .... An important factor in the success of these is the small **39** .... Also, the element of **40** .... is usually present, which contributes greatly.

Youth

Unit aims

Listening skills

Understanding maps
Sentence and table completion

Speaking skills

Describing jobs
Advantages and disadvantages
Pronunciation: compound adjectives

Topic talk

1   Look at the job advertisement below and answer the questions which follow.

> ### Youth worker required
>
> Must be articulate, prepared to learn, energetic, responsible, and highly-motivated.
>
> At least two years' experience of youth work essential.
>
> Immediate start.
>
> Salary to be negotiated.

a   Is the above job more suitable for a younger or an older person? Give reasons for your answer.
b   Why do you think the person needs to be energetic, responsible, and highly-motivated?
c   Would you apply for a job like this? Why? Why not?

2   In different parts of the IELTS Listening and Speaking tests, you may need to consider the attributes required for different jobs. Match each criterion 1–9 with a list of adjectives a–i. The first one has been done for you.

1   appearance .....*c*.....
2   intellectual ability
3   maturity of outlook
4   interpersonal skills
5   communication skills
6   willingness to learn
7   qualifications
8   attitude to work
9   skills and general ability

a   sociable, friendly, likeable, personable
b   articulate, outgoing, communicative, well-spoken
c   well-dressed, neat, well-groomed, elegant
d   conscientious, hardworking, dependable, reliable
e   well-qualified, computer-literate, well-trained
f   bright, quick, clever, intelligent
g   skilled, able, capable, experienced
h   responsible, mature, grown-up, independent
i   enthusiastic, eager, dynamic, adaptable, flexible

3   Add each of the adjectives below to the appropriate list a–i in 2.

> trustworthy   lively   accomplished   approachable   smart   adult
> well-mannered   educated

4   The adjectives in the list below are opposites of those in the lists in 2. Match each adjective with its opposite.

> apathetic   careless   childish   inarticulate   scruffy   slow
> uneducated   unfriendly   inexperienced

5   Questions are often divided into open and closed categories. Closed questions can be answered *yes* or *no*, whereas open questions require a fuller answer. Divide questions a–h below into these two categories.

a   Does a young worker nowadays need to be more qualified than in the past?
b   Are young people more or less interested in finding a career than in the past?
c   What difficulties do young people face in the changing world we live in?
d   Do you generally find job interviews difficult?
e   How do you think the work environment will be changed for future generations of young people?
f   What can be done to overcome these difficulties?
g   How does this differ from the past?
h   Why? Why not?

6   In which part of the Speaking test, Part 1 or Part 3, would you expect to find the questions in 5?

7   Decide which questions in 5 could be answered beginning with the phrases below.

There are many problems, but perhaps the greatest challenge is …
The most likely development is that …
By far the best way to tackle the situation is … because …
The main difference is …

8   With a partner, ask and answer the questions in 5. Use the phrases in 7. Then develop your answers by using the following words to trigger and organize your ideas.

> As a result,   This is because   Firstly,   But perhaps the best solution is to
> Another point that will stand out is   This means that

Listening skills   Understanding maps

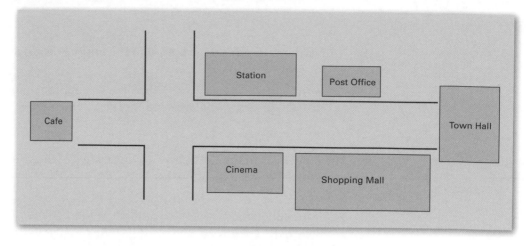

1   Look at the map and answer the questions.

  a   What is between the station and the town hall?
  b   What is opposite the post office?
  c   What is next to the cinema?

2   Look at the map again and match the sentence halves below to make true statements.

  1   As you go into the station
  2   From the town hall
  3   As you face the town hall
  4   From the cafe
  5   Standing facing the cafe
  6   As you come out of the station

  a   the town hall is behind you.
  b   the cinema is in front of you.
  c   the post office is on your right.
  d   the post office is on your left.
  e   the post office is further away than the station.
  f   the cinema is further away than the shopping mall.

3   Match the uses of *right* in these sentences with the correct meaning.

  1   The cinema is right in front of you.
  2   The post office is the right place to buy stamps.
  3   Coming from the cafe, the shopping mall is on your right.

  a   correct
  b   opposite of left
  c   directly, immediately

4   The plan on the next page is taken from a map labelling task. Look at the plan and answer the questions a–d.

  a   Where is question 1 in relation to the breakfast tent?
  b   Where is question 2 in relation to Campsite 1 and the disabled viewing?
  c   Where is question 3 in relation to the stage and the Olde England Pub?
  d   Where is question 3 in relation to the disabled viewing?

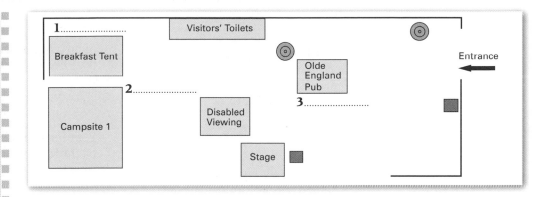

5 1.24 Listen to the first part of the recording and label the plan. Write the correct letters A–F next to questions 1–3 on the map.

A small security office	D staff toilets
B main security office	E staff meeting point
C first aid tent	F visitors' meeting point

Sentence and table completion

6 Read the sentence and table completion questions which follow on from the map labelling task above. Then answer questions a–c below.

a What is the general theme of questions 4–6?
b Which questions in 4–6 relate to an event, a place, and a thing?
c Which answers in the table are to some extent predictable?

Complete the sentences below.
Write **NO MORE THAN TWO WORDS** *for each answer.*

4 In the first year, it was a .... , and not a real festival.

5 Shortly afterwards the event was moved, and the .... was in the background.

6 Now the festival is held in the ....

Complete the table below.
Write **NO MORE THAN TWO WORDS AND/OR A NUMBER** *for each answer.*

	Children's Zone team	Security team	First aid team
Meeting place	In Campsite 2	Behind the stage	**8** At the ....
Meeting time	2 p.m.	**7** .... p.m.	4 p.m.
Final meeting time for all teams		**9** .... a.m.	
Final meeting place for all teams		**10**	

7 1.25 Listen to the second part of the recording and answer the questions 4–10 in 6.

1   Read the small job advertisements below and answer questions a–e.

> Men and women wanted for modelling. No experience necessary. Contracts with TV and magazines. £££
> Phone **0789 345213**

> Fill envelopes at home. £4.50 per 100. Phone 0766 657291

> Door-to-door kitchen salespeople wanted. Pay according to results. Phone 0798 864233

> Waiters/waitresses wanted. Night work. Good pay plus tips. Phone **0796 975779**

a   Are these careers or jobs?
b   What, in your view, is the difference between a job and a career?
c   Which of these jobs is suitable for a student?
d   Which of these jobs would you be willing to do as a student?
e   What are the jobs that students do in your country?

2   Number the jobs in the list below according to how well-paid they are (1 = highest paid; 4 = lowest paid) and according to how socially useful they are (1 = most useful; 4 = least useful).

> bus-driver   dentist   shop assistant   pop star

3   Answer these questions about your answers in 2.

a   Is the situation fair? Should the situation be different?
b   Should governments try to change the situation?

4   What features from the list would you associate with each job a–h?

a   architect
b   nurse
c   company director
d   politician
e   doctor
f   schoolteacher
g   chef
h   footballer

> risk   excitement   social prestige   long holidays   long training
> high job satisfaction   variety of job activities   high pay
> good pension   social usefulness   expensive training

Advantages and disadvantages

5 1.26 Listen to three people talking about jobs and answer the questions.

a   Which of them talk about working while studying?
b   Which of them talk about their own full-time job?
c   Which of them do not believe that working while studying is a good thing?

6 1.26 Answer questions a–i below with phrases from the list. Then listen again to the people speaking to check your answers.

First speaker

a   What words does he use to refer to advantages and disadvantages?

....

b   Which two phrases does he use to indicate a contrast?

....

c   How does he introduce his conclusion?

....

Second speaker

d   How does she introduce the disadvantages of her job?

....

e   How does she introduce the advantages of her job?

....

f   What word does she use to present her conclusion?

....

Third speaker

g   What phrase does she use instead of the *advantage*?

....

h   What phrase does she use instead of the *disadvantage*?

....

i   How does she introduce her conclusion?

....

> the minus   the disadvantage with ... is that   weighing everything up
> the plus   on the other   cons   overall   pros   on balance
> the great advantage is that   on the one hand

7 The ideas in the list below relate to the Speaking Part 3 question: *Is it better to go travelling on your own or with other people?* Which ideas relate to travelling alone? Which relate to travelling with others?

a   easier to meet new friends
b   free to go where you please
c   complete control of your money
d   you must make group decisions
e   more safety in numbers
f   cheaper to share things
g   you may get lonely
h   you can stay extra time in places as you want
i   more fun

8 With a partner, give your own answer to the question in 7. Use the expressions in the phrase banks below to help you.

Phrase bank

Advantages
One definite plus is that
The great advantage is

Disadvantages
One problem is that
Another big disadvantage is
A big minus is

Balancing
Weighing everything up,
On balance,
Taking everything into account,

9 With a partner, ask and answer these Speaking Part 3 questions.

a Is it a good idea to take a gap year after university and before starting a job?
b When people are studying at university, is it better for them to live at home or to move away from their families?
c Which is more important in a job, money or job satisfaction?
d Which are more useful in helping people to relax – mental activities or physical activities?

Pronunciation: compound adjectives

10 Answer these questions.

a How long does it take you to make yourself *well-dressed* or *well-groomed*?
b How long does it take to become *well-travelled* or *well-qualified*?

11 1.27 Listen to the pairs of sentences. Where is the stress on *hard-working* and *well-paid* in the sentences?

a Jack is a very *hard-working* manager.
All Dixon's store managers are *hard-working*.
b Jack is a *well-paid* accountant.
Most accountants are *well-paid*.

12 What can you say about the stress on words like *well-paid* in these situation?

a when they are used before a noun
b when they are used on their own or after a verb

13 Think of people you know. For each of the adjectives below, write two sentences about the person, changing the position of the adjective. Then practise saying your sentences.

well-mannered
fully-trained
smartly-dressed
fair-minded
easy-going

Exam listening

Section 1

 1.28

Questions 1–3

Label the map.
Choose answers from the list below. Write the correct letter's **A–H** *on the map.*

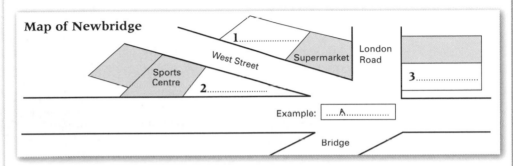

Map of Newbridge

A	High Street (*example*)	E	The Heights
B	tennis courts	F	railway station
C	car park	G	town hall
D	The Towers	H	bus station

 1.29

Questions 4–8

Write the appropriate letters **A–C** *against the flat numbers.*

What is the next thing the student should do?

A   apply to an agency
B   deal through the accommodation officer
C   apply directly to the owner

4	Flat 4	....
5	Flat 6	....
6	Flat 8	....
7	Flat 10	....
8	Flat 14	....

Questions 9 and 10

Complete the sentences below.
Write **NO MORE THAN TWO WORDS** *for each answer.*

The biggest employers in Newbridge used to be **9** ....

There is little student accommodation in the **10** .... around the town.

Culture

Unit aims

Listening skills   Speaking skills

Understanding layout   Free time activities
Predicting from notes   Expressing preferences
                                    Dealing with unfamiliar questions
                                    Pronunciation: *like* and *'d like*

Topic talk

1   Look at the photo and answer the
    questions.

    a   To what extent do buildings
        reflect the culture of a country?
    b   How important is it to keep old
        buildings?
    c   Which buildings are famous in
        your country?
    d   How can we keep traditional
        buildings and still make progress?

2   In the IELTS Speaking test, it
    is important to understand the
    questions the examiner is asking. In
    questions a–g, put the words in italic
    into the correct order.

    a   *are / buildings / how / modern /
        popular* in your country? Why?
    b   *same / architecture / is / the / the / as /
        here* in your home country?
    c   *traditional / you / do / prefer / or /
        modern* architecture? Why?
    d   *any / there / of / which / kind / is /
        building* you don't like? Why?
    e   *you / buildings / special / have / of
        / significance / any / do* in your
        country?
    f   *changed / type / the / of / building / has* since you were a child? How?
    g   *building / kinds / of / what* appeal to you most? Why?

3   Decide which responses 1–7 below you would use to answer questions a–g
    in 2.

    1   I'm not too keen on tall structures like skyscrapers.
    2   There are lots like the Parthenon.
    3   I think I like more contemporary designs better.
    4   Not at all. In fact, it couldn't be more different.
    5   Buildings with lots of glass.
    6   Only in recent years.
    7   I'd say they are very much in fashion at the moment.

4 Match the responses 1–7 in 3 with the explanations below which develop the answers.

a as new houses are appearing everywhere and old houses are being pulled down.
b because there are fewer mega-structures here, while in my country they are everywhere.
c because high buildings make me dizzy. I prefer buildings with three or four storeys.
d as old-fashioned buildings are dull and often a bit scary.
e which reflect the culture of the country and bring in tourists.
f as there was no money before, while now there's lots of investment.
g since they're brighter, which makes them more airy and cheerful.

5 With a partner, practise asking and answering the questions in 2.

6 In Speaking Part 1, you may be asked to talk about your preferences. Complete sentences a–g with the words below.

> hate   adore   would rather   prefer   stand   appeal   dislike

a I don't .... modern architecture, but I do think that there are many examples that are very ugly.
b I .... live in town than in the countryside.
c I am fond of old family houses, but I .... much more modern ones.
d I can't .... old films except for early comedies.
e Books .... to me as much as music.
f While some people simply .... the theatre, I am indifferent to it.
g I don't .... literature. It's just that I don't have much time for reading.

7 With a partner, express your preference out of each of the pairs of items below. Use the verbs in 6 and explain your decisions.

a contemporary books *or* classic literature
b plays in the theatre *or* outdoor drama
c films on DVD *or* films in the cinema
d urban living *or* country life
e popular *or* classical music
f keeping a diary *or* writing a blog
g art films *or* Hollywood blockbusters

1   Two students attended a lecture on the attitudes of young people. Read the two sets of notes that the students took. Then answer the questions below.

A

purpose of study

values among students

sample size

500 boys

aged 15

500 girls

same age

survey type

questions and answers

items in survey

money

fashion

success

B

Values among young people

Purpose of study   a   identification of values held by boys and girls

                           b   differences between the two groups

Sample type   boys and girls (500 of each)

                                15 years

Name of study   <u>relative</u> values among adolescents

Survey type   Questionnaire

                                Answers on scale 1–7

Items in survey

- money
- fashion
- success

a   Which arrangement of notes is easier to understand?

b   Which of the following are used to assist in the clear layout of the notes? Identify where they are used.

italic type	bold	indentation	numbering / lettering	bullet points
	capitals	underlining	headings / titles	

2   Organize these notes about the country of Fiji in a clear and logical format. Use some of the features in 1.

capital	English	Fiji	official language	Suva	sugar	hot and wet
population	ethnic composition	Fijian	coconuts	resources		
Asian Indian	gold	800,000	crops	climate	name of country	

Predicting from notes

3   The notes below are taken from a note completion task based on a lecture. Read the notes and answer these questions.

a   What is the title of the lecture?
b   How many parts are there in the lecture?
c   What is the subject of each part?
d   How does the lecture end?
e   What information can you predict for each space?

4   2.1 Listen to the recording and complete the notes. Write NO MORE THAN TWO WORDS AND/OR A NUMBER for each answer.

Culture and Society

Study: 2004

on the global teenager hypothesis (i.e. values of teenagers in the world are similar)

Is there a global culture?

One special aspect of the study: **1** .... in three cultures

Sample: **2** .... high school students

14–17 years

Three countries: China, Japan, USA

Questionnaire: number of statements: **3** ....

Three examples of statements:

Statement 1   It is really true that **4** .... can make you happy.

Statement 2   My dream in life is to be able to own **5** ....

Statement 5   Having the right **6** .... is the most important thing in life.

Examples of results

Statement 1   nationality which agreed most strongly: **7** ....

Statement 2   nationality which agreed most strongly: **8** ....

Statement 5   nationality which agreed most strongly: **9** ....

General conclusion

The global teenager hypothesis is **10** .... by this research.

More research needed!

Speaking skills   Free time activities

1   Read these two diaries written by the same person and answer questions a–d.

Saturday 16 March

a.m.	11.00	meet Ken in town – coffee
p.m.	2.30	golf with David at club
eve	7.30	cinema: Pirates of the Caribbean 2. Meet the girls at 7.00 in the usual place.

Saturday 16 March

Ken was delayed so did shopping at the supermarket. Met him for lunch – he paid! Big rush to get to the club in time. David had brought Bill and Charlotte. We all played. I need a lot more practice! Only Janet arrived for the movie, so we went to see *Snakes on a Plane* instead. Great fun, probably better than *Pirates*, I imagine.

a   What are the differences between the two diaries?
b   Do you think her day was better than she had planned or not?
c   Is it better to make detailed plans for the future or to leave some things to chance?
d   What can be the disadvantages of planning ahead?

2   Put the leisure activities in the list into three groups 1–3.

1   Sports
2   Hobbies
3   Social activities

> golf   ice hockey   chess   stamp-collecting   meeting friends
> tennis   gardening   going to concerts   going to parties
> chatting on the phone   football   shopping

3   In Speaking Part 1, you may be asked about your leisure activities. Answer these questions about the activities in 2.

a   Which of these, if any, do you like doing?
b   Are there other activities, hobbies, or sports which take up a lot of your time?
c   To what extent do you plan how and when you do them?

Expressing preferences

4   2.2 Listen to three people talking about what they like doing in their free time. Complete the table below with the activities they like doing? Which is their favourite?

	Activities	Favourite
Speaker 1:	....	....
Speaker 2:	....	....
Speaker 3:	....	....

5 2.2 Complete the lists of expressions below for expressing and explaining preferences. Listen again to the people talking and fill in the gaps.

Phrase bank

Expressing preferences

I .... listening to music.

I .... gardening.

My .... thing of all is going to the theatre.

Best of .... , I like gardening.

Explaining preferences

What .... me .... is that …

I can do it .... fun or ....

I .... it relaxing.

.... thing I .... gardening is that …

And .... other .... is that I can …

That's .... thing about …

6 With a partner, ask and answer the Speaking Part 1 questions below, using the expressions in the list above to help you.

a How do you spend your weekends?
b What else do you like doing in your free time?

Dealing with unfamiliar topics

7 Which activities below do you know something about? Which do you know little about?

playing a musical instrument painting cookery games

8 Match each question 1–4 with an answer a–d.

1 Are you able to play any musical instruments?
2 Do you have any artistic abilities?
3 What sort of food do you enjoy cooking and eating?
4 Which games do you enjoy playing?

a I'm afraid I have absolutely no skill in this area at all. But I might learn in the future. It is simply too expensive to live on fast food.
b That's not something I normally do. I probably used to when I was a lot younger, but my life's very busy now.
c Unfortunately not. I have very little practical ability, and things like that are difficult for me. I tried when I was at school, but without success.
d I wish I could. My parents made me take lessons when I was very young, but I just made a terrible noise and they let me give it up. I don't think I have any ability in that direction.

Technique

In Speaking Part 1, you will normally be asked about familiar topics, but sometimes the questions may involve areas in which you have no experience. Say why it is difficult to answer. Try to explain your personal situation.

9 Answer these questions about the responses in 8.

a   What do all four responses have in common?
b   Which answers refer to past experience, natural ability, or future hopes?
c   Which expressions does each speaker use to say 'no'?

10 With a partner, practise asking and answering these questions, which may be difficult for some candidates. Use the expressions you identified in 9.

a   Are you interested in drawing?
b   Do you like singing?
c   Can you dance?
d   Are you good at making things?

11 With a partner, ask and answer this typical Speaking Part 1 question sequence.

a   Do you have any hobbies?
b   How and why did you first get involved in this activity?
c   How would you recommend it to another person?

Pronunciation: *like* and *'d like*

12 Read sentences a–c. Which sentences indicate a present intention? something the speaker enjoys doing? something the speaker feels they should do?

a   I'd like to try a new hobby.
b   I like to visit the dentist twice a year.
c   I like listening to rock music.

13 2.3 Listen to the sentences on the recording and fill in the gaps with *like* or *'d like*.

a   … to have coffee at eleven.
b   … to have coffee at eleven.
c   … to redecorate my house to make it look beautiful.
d   … to redecorate my house to make it look beautiful.
e   … to get up early.
f   … to get up early.

14 Practise saying aloud the sentences in 12.

15 Complete the dialogue using the correct form of *like* or *'d like*. Then practise the dialogue aloud.

David   Do you take golf lessons to improve your game?

Susan   Oh yes. I .... to take lessons if I have the time, but I ....
            playing the game even more!

David   Do you have any ambition in golf?

Susan   Yes. I .... to win the annual championship at my club!

Exam listening

Section 3

Questions 21–26 **2.4**

Choose the correct letter **A**, **B**, *or* **C**.

21 What is the main topic of the assignment?

  A the historical development of television

  B the development of new media

  C the cultural future of television

22 According to Emilie, which new technology will become the biggest competition for television?

  A iPods

  B mobile phones

  C video games

23 According to the tutor, the average length of a television programme might become

  A 45 minutes.

  B four to five minutes.

  C ten minutes.

24 What part of the library is going to be closed for one week?

  A the Sociology section

  B the Media Studies section

  C the Journals section

25 Which body do they decide to complain to?

  A the Premises Committee

  B the Students' Union

  C the library

26 What will the reprographics office do?

  A send emails to your tutor

  B send your dissertation to you

  C send your dissertation to your tutor

Questions 27–30 **2.5**

Write **NO MORE THAN THREE WORDS AND/OR A NUMBER** *for each answer.*

27 What does the tutor compare homemade videos with?

  ....

28 What is the title of Mrs Jones's lecture?

  ....

29 Where is the lecture?

  ....

30 When is the final date for the assignment?

  ....

Arts and Sciences

Unit aims

Listening skills

Questions from statements
Paraphrases for matching

Speaking skills

Comparing and evaluating
Expressing others' views
Pronunciation: weak forms

Topic talk

1 Look at the photo below and answer the questions.

a   Do you think that artists and scientists are born or are they made? Why? Why not?
b   Do you think it is possible for students to combine both the arts and sciences at school or university? Why? Why not?
c   What made you choose the subject you are studying? If you could, would you change your mind now?

2 Decide which adjective best matches the descriptions a–i below.

Example

a   *ostentatious*

original   talented   rigorous   curious   accomplished   ostentatious
expressive   impartial   creative

a   He's very pretentious and likes to show everyone how rich he is.
b   He plays the violin so well.
c   His approach to experiments is very precise and methodical.
d   She may be a budding artist but her work is very avant-garde and has never been seen before.
e   She has been described as a very gifted and ingenious sculptor.
f   His poems are very moving as they show his emotions clearly.
g   He has to be neutral in his work and cannot allow his emotions to take over.
h   His books are full of original ideas.
i   Even as a young chemist she had a very inquiring mind and investigated everything thoroughly.

3 Write the noun form for each adjective in 2.

Example

ostentatious   *ostentation*

4   With a partner, choose five nouns or adjectives from 2 and 3 above and explain why the qualities are necessary. Give your own reasons.

Example

Why does an artist need to be talented/have talent?
Someone who is involved in the arts has to have talent, because …

5   In the IELTS Listening test, you may have to listen to someone talking about rules, procedures, or guidelines. Look at the list below and decide what the speaker is talking about in a–h.

Example

And finally you have to have the application in by the end of the week.
assignment deadline

> assignment deadline   application   assignment guidelines
> society/club constitution   hall of residence regulations
> set of instructions   examination rules and regulations
> assessment criteria

a   You must be in by midnight, as the doors are locked. You must then call the porter.
b   When the final bell rings, you must put your pens down immediately.
c   The essay on Fine Art needs to be typed and bound.
d   The use of PowerPoint is a must. Your physics experiment will be marked on your presentation.
e   It is essential that members follow the rules at all times.
f   All you need to know about how to do this is contained in this booklet.
g   All history essays must be handed in by noon on Friday.
h   When you send the form, two photographs need to be included.

6   Decide which of the following words mean the same as *compulsory*.

> not optional   mandatory   certain   obligatory   possible
> requisite   vital   imperative   crucial

7   Work with a partner and give your own explanation for the questions below. In each case, use two of the following phrases in your answer: *in order to, because, for example, like,* or *if.*

a   Why is it necessary to present assignments well in all disciplines?
b   What is the effect of visuals in a presentation? Do you think they should be compulsory even in essays?
d   What is the benefit of a bibliography when you produce an essay?
e   Why is preparation for any assignment crucial?
f   Is writing a draft of an essay or report essential? Why? Why not?
g   What in your opinion is the key to preparing a good assignment?
h   What qualities do you need to show when you are making a presentation of your work?

Listening skills   Questions from statements

1   The questions below are taken from a multiple-choice task. Read questions 1–5 carefully and answer the questions below.

    a   What general topic is being discussed?

    b   What group of people are probably being addressed?

2   Some of the question stems are phrased as statements. Rephrase each statement as a question.

Example

Teachers visiting a festival should arrive at …
When should teachers visiting the festival arrive?

Questions 1–5

Choose the correct letter **A**, **B**, *or* **C**.

1   What will the head of science probably do?

    A   arrange the visit to the festival

    B   confirm the school placements

    C   provide information about the festival

2   The student teachers should arrange visits that last

    A   one or two days.

    B   two or three days.

    C   all three days.

3   The most important purpose of festival visits is to

    A   get better exam grades.

    B   create enthusiasm for science.

    C   enable students to have fun.

4   The central features of our scientific age are

    A   inventions and improvements.

    B   interesting and unusual events.

    C   interest and enthusiasm for science.

5   What kind of specialists are teaching maths?

    A   physicists

    B   biologists

    C   chemists

---

3   2.6 Listen to the recording and answer questions 1–5 above.

Paraphrases for matching

4 Read the extract below from a review of the book *Science in our World*.
Match each chapter subject a–e with the chapter numbers 1–5.

Technique

Predict the words or phrases you might hear in matching tasks by thinking of synonyms or paraphrases for options given.

> Chapter 1 concerns the purpose of science in the early days, namely to foretell the future by studying the stars. Science has had a long journey through the past centuries and this story is told in Chapter 2. The catastrophes that science has caused in the world are dealt with in Chapter 3. Some biographies of the celebrated names of science are given in Chapter 4. Finally, the innovations that science has brought to our lives are covered in Chapter 5.

Science in our World
Contents

Chapter 1:	a	*history* of science
Chapter 2:	b	*famous* scientists
Chapter 3:	c	*astrology* and science
Chapter 4:	d	*new things* from science
Chapter 5:	e	scientific *disasters*

5 Underline synonyms or paraphrases in the extract which match the words in italic in a–e above.

6 The questions below are taken from a matching task. Read the questions and options carefully, then answer questions a–d below.

A   a show
B   an event of local interest
C   a technical demonstration
D   an open discussion
E   an interactive event

6   Waterworld ....
7   Transport 2050 ....
8   Science in a suitcase ....
9   Ropes and hangings ....
10 Paper and time ....

---

a   What kinds of options are given in A–E?
b   What do the capital letters in 6–10 tell you?
c   Which list do you expect to be paraphrased in the recording?
d   Which words or expressions might be used by the speakers to paraphrase this list? Make a list for each item.

7 2.7 Listen to the recording and answer the questions in 6. Write the correct letters A–E next to the questions 6–10.

1   Read the short texts below and answer the questions.

> The sculptor made a laughing head. He put it on a stand and entered it for the modern art competition. The head became separated from the stand. This left the stand and a little stick of wood on the top. The judges never saw the head, but the stand and stick of wood was presented to them and they awarded it a prize. The sculptor was surprised but very happy.

> He was quickly cleaning up his laboratory and put an old dish of liquid on a window shelf. He locked up and went home. A few weeks later he remembered the dish and looked at it. Then he saw something unusual about the liquid. And so penicillin was born!

a   What was the accident that happened in each case? What was the result of each accident?

b   Which are more important – the accidents of science or the accidents of art?

2   Separate the words into two lists: words associated with the arts and words associated with the sciences.

Arts   ....

Sciences   ....

> numeracy   knowledge of humanity   performance   analytical   creative
> demonstration   discipline   mysterious   knowledge of the universe
> experiment   certainty   literacy   incremental   work of art
> imagination   original   definite   uncertainty

3   Answer these questions about the lists you made in 2.

a   Which words were difficult to categorize?

b   Can you think of examples to justify applying some science words to the arts and vice versa?

4   Read the three typical Speaking Part 3 questions below. Which questions require a *comparison* in response? Which require an *evaluation*?

a   Which provides the best entertainment: a novel or a film?

b   To what extent have people's lives been improved by science?

c   To what degree are our lives improved by the arts?

d   Which is more important in modern cultures: scientific or artistic ability?

5 Phrases 1–6 below can be used to answer the questions in 4. Match each phrase with a question in 4.

1 I think it's had a huge/minor influence. For example, …

2 This depends on whether you prefer …

3 To quite a large degree, because …

4 In my opinion, … is the most …

5 I think … is more important because …

6 I (don't) think it's a crucial factor because …

6 With a partner, ask and answer the questions in 4, using the phrases above to answer.

Expressing others' views

7 Some students expressed these opinions about science and the arts. Read their statements and decide whether you agree or disagree. Change the opinions so that they express your views.

> Science has the ability to make all our lives much easier.

> The arts teach us what it means to be human.

> Most of the arts are of no practical use and are a waste of time.

> Science will certainly lead the world to disaster.

8 2.8 Listen to three speakers answer Speaking Part 3 questions. Match each speaker with the correct question a–c.

Speaker 1: ....

Speaker 2: ....

Speaker 3: ....

a To what extent should the arts be sponsored by government?
b Why do you think some people are distrustful of science?
c How can new technology help in our domestic lives?

9 Which of these arguments does each speaker agree with?

a Technology just creates more work.
b The arts contribute to society.
c Technology makes tasks easier.
d Scientists aren't engaged with the world.
e The arts should be more commercial.
f Scientists understand the impact of their ideas.

10 2.8 Listen to the three speakers again. Check your answers to 9 and complete the table below with the phrases each speaker uses to introduce other people's opinions.

Other people's opinions

Speaker 1: ....

Speaker 2: ....

Speaker 3: ....

11 2.8 Listen a final time. Make a note of the phrases the speakers use to disagree with other people's opinions.

Disagreeing

Speaker 1: ....

Speaker 2: ....

Speaker 3: ....

12 With a partner, ask and answer the Speaking Part 3 question sequences below. Use the phrases in 10 and 11 to introduce other views and your own.

Sequence 1

a   Should governments subsidize scientific research? Why?

b   Which is more important in our society today, the sciences or the arts?

c   What harm can science do to us?

Sequence 2

a   How big a part do machines play in our lives today?

b   What are some of the problems with being so dependent on machines?

c   To what extent would it be better to lead a simpler life, without advanced technology?

Pronunciation: weak forms

13 2.9 Listen to the phrase below. How is *the* pronounced differently? Why does this happen?

the arts and the sciences

14 2.10 In each of the following sentences, the words in italic are pronounced in two different ways. Circle the word which is not stressed. Underline the word which is stressed. Listen to the recording and check.

a   People say *that* science will provide the solutions to all our problems, but I don't think *that* outcome is very likely.

b   *There* are many inventions which came from China in the distant past, and now a lot of brilliant scientists are working *there*.

c   *Some* scientific inventions have resulted in great harm; others have resulted in *some* useful labour-saving products.

15 Practise saying the sentences in 14.

Exam listening

Section 3

 2.11

Questions 21–25

Complete the notes below.
*Write **NO MORE THAN THREE WORDS OR A NUMBER** for each answer.*

The Arts Association receives **21** £ .... million from the government.

The first issue the Arts Association tries to address is **22** ....

All the issues mean that the arts are for **23** ....

The government wants **24** .... in return for its contribution.

The **25** .... programme helps organizations with financial problems.

2.12

Questions 26–30

What is the subject of each of the books Mr Simpson recommended to Arthur?
*Choose your answers from the box and write the letters **A–F** next to the question numbers.*

A   financial information

B   psychology of art

C   art and other media

D   modern art

E   history of art

F   the art market

Greenberg	**26** ....
Parliamentary report	**27** ....
Dennison	**28** ....
Hampton	**29** ....
Frick	**30** ....

Nature

Unit aims

Listening skills

Changing opinions
Extended multiple choice
Summary completion (2)

Speaking skills

Describing animals
Describing presents
Making notes

Topic talk

1 Look at the photo below and answer the questions which follow.

a   Do you find places like the scene in the picture beautiful or boring?
b   Why are places like this attractive to people?
c   Why do we need places like this more and more in the modern world?

2 Decide whether the statements below show the speaker is enthusiastic or unenthusiastic about a place.

a   The holiday cottage caught my attention immediately, so I bought it.
b   I have been fascinated by the building since I first saw it.
c   As it's in the middle of nowhere, it's very peaceful.
d   The house is basically okay.
e   Living in such a remote area is just about bearable.
f   Even though it's in the middle of the city, it's not at all noisy.
g   What makes the place so attractive is the open fields.
h   The reason why it appeals to me is the sound of the crashing waves at night.

3 Add the following phrases to as many of the sentences a–h above as you can.

Example

a   *2; 5*

1   but it's in danger of being spoilt by tourists visiting it.
2   but sadly I haven't visited it for years.
3   In fact, at times it's quieter than the countryside.
4   but I'm afraid that won't last long.
5   but at times it can be lonely there.

4 Read the examples below. Then rewrite sentences a–g, beginning with *what*.

Examples

The open fields make the place so attractive.
What makes the place so attractive is the open fields.
The house is quiet because there are no neighbours.
What makes the house quiet is not having (any) neighbours.

a   The silence there makes me feel so relaxed.
b   Being away from the city does me a lot of good.
c   The place is restful because there are no shops.
d   The sea is clean because there are no factories.
e   The trees make the garden very private.
f   The people make the area so welcoming.
g   The area is appealing because it has many tourist attractions.

5 With a partner, practise asking questions beginning with *why* based on the statements in 4. Then answer with sentences beginning with *what*.

Example

Why is the place so relaxing?
What makes me relaxed there is the silence.

6 In Speaking Part 2, you may be asked to talk about a place or something else from your personal experience. Complete each of the statements below with an example from your own life.

a   The building that I like most is …
b   The pet I remember best is …
c   The present I will never forget was …
d   The incident that embarrassed me most was …
e   One holiday I will never forget was …
f   A school trip I remember well was …

7 Write a follow-up sentence with *what* to develop each of the ideas in 6.

Example

What I like most about the building is the large windows.

8 With a partner, describe the experiences in 6. Start with your sentences. Then develop your ideas using the words below.

| because | as | since | with | which |

1   Read the four dialogues below.

  a   Which speakers change their minds?

  b   What phrases do they use to indicate this?

1

A   What river's that?

B   That's the River Exe, no, I mean the River Avon.

2

C   Ben Nevis is the tallest mountain in Scotland. In the UK, in fact.

D   Really?

3

E   If we leave now, we will see the sunset.

F   I'm not so sure about that. The sky looks very cloudy.

E   Actually, you're right. It might be better to wait until another day.

4

G   If we visit the lake this afternoon, we may see the ducks flying in.

H   I think you'll find they come in greater numbers in the evening.

G   Yes, that's what I meant, in the evening. We'll see thousands in the evening.

2   Read the dialogue. Then answer questions a–c below.

Man	What shall we do this morning? We can visit the monkeys first – they're always fun.
Woman	But the monkeys will be having their tea-party in the afternoon. That will be the best time to see them.
Man	Well, we can see the elephants, then.
Woman	The keepers bring *them* out after midday too.
Man	Then we should visit the aquarium – the fish are always awake.
Woman	That's a good idea. We'll see the fish. And what about the bears?
Man	The bears' cages are not open today, although we can see the polar bears this morning if we want.
Woman	Yes, let's see those and the fish. And then we can have lunch.
Man	All right. Let's go.

  a   How many animals do they talk about visiting?

  b   How many animals do they decide to visit?

  c   At what stage in the conversation do you know their decision: the beginning, the middle, or the end?

Technique

In extended multiple-choice questions, you may hear most or all of the options on the recording. Don't just select the first words you hear. Speakers may change their minds, so you cannot answer the question with certainty until the discussion is finished.

Extended multiple choice

3   The questions below come from an extended multiple-choice task. How many selections must you make for each?

Questions 1–3

Choose THREE letters **A–G**.

What topics must the assignment cover?

A   zoo finances

B   public safety

C   the history of zoos

D   animal welfare

E   education and zoos

F   zoos for science

G   value for money

Questions 4 and 5

Choose TWO letters **A–E**.

Which areas do the students decide to concentrate their efforts on?

A   science

B   history

C   entertainment

D   conservation

E   education

4   2.13 Listen to the first part of the recording and answer questions 1–5.

Summary completion (2)

5   The paragraph below is taken from a summary completion task. Read the paragraph and decide what kind of information is missing in each question. Match each space 6–10 with a word from the list.

an activity	a person	a date	a number	a place	a colour
		an adjective			

The Arabian oryx is mainly **6** .... in colour. It lives in a **7** ....

climate. In **8** .... it became extinct. Now, there are about **9** ....

in Oman. A crash in the population was caused by **10** ....

6   2.14 Listen to the second part of the recording and complete the summary. Write NO MORE THAN THREE WORDS AND/OR A NUMBER for each answer.

Speaking skills   Describing animals

1 Read the short texts in which people talk about pets they had as children. Match each description a–c with an animal from the list.

| cat   parrot   dog   rabbit   horse   goldfish   mouse |

a

We had him for about ten years. I grew up with him, I suppose. He was always very lively when someone new arrived at the house, jumping up and wagging his tail. The fondest memory I have is of taking him for walks along the canal. I also enjoyed throwing a stick for him in the park. When he was happy he'd bark a lot. I really miss him.

b

She was quite a character. I wouldn't say she was friendly – far from it in fact. She had a habit of arching her back and scratching people she didn't take a liking to. But what I remember most is letting her curl up on my lap, and then stroking her. I'm not sure who found it the most relaxing, me or her. She certainly liked it, and she always purred very loudly.

c

Looking after her involved quite a lot of work. We used to have to go to the farm every night with a bale of hay to feed her. I also used to groom her, which was fun, but hard work. So it was all quite tough, but worth it in the end. The thing that sticks in my mind is the way she used to get excited just before we started jumping. They were very happy times.

2 Read the descriptions again. Complete the first column of the table below with the name of the animal. Then write verbs typical of that animal in the second column. The first one has been done for you.

Animal	Typical actions	Human actions
a	*jump up*	....
b	....	....
c	....	....

3 Complete the third column with verbs that describe what people typically do with these animals, for example, *take them for walks*.

4 Each text in 1 contains a phrase for introducing a memory. Underline these phrases.

5 2.15 Listen to three people talking about animals and pets. Decide which speaker is answering which question below.

a   What was your pet like?
b   Have you ever had a favourite pet?
c   What was your favourite pet animal when you were a child?

6 2.15 Listen again. What phrase does each speaker use to show he/she does not regard the animal as a pet?

Speaker 1:   Although .... a pet, ...

Speaker 2:   I'm .... is a real pet.

Speaker 3:   .... , he wasn't my pet at all.

7 The taskcard below is taken from **Speaking Part 2**. Take one minute to think and make notes about your own talk on this topic, using your own experience. Then practise speaking for two minutes using your notes.

Describe an animal which belonged to you or someone you know.

You should say

what type of animal it was

what personality it had

what it typically did

and explain your own personal reaction to it.

Describing presents

8 Read the following slogan from a public information campaign. Then answer questions a–c below.

A pet is for life, not just for Christmas.

a   What do you think the campaign is about?
b   Do you think animals make good gifts?
c   What questions should you ask yourself before you give a gift like this?

9 The list below gives common occasions on which people give presents. Answer questions a–c below.

wedding   birthday   wedding anniversary   religious festival
moving house   leaving a job   visiting a friend's home

a   On which of these occasions do you give presents in your country?
b   Are there any other occasions on which you give presents?
c   What presents are suitable for each occasion?

10 Read these two articles about present giving. Then answer questions a–c below.

Present madness

The greetings card industry is making more and more money every year. There are so many occasions on which we must give greetings cards now. Mother's Day and Father's Day require cards and presents from all to all. Soon, I firmly believe, we will have Brother's, Sister's, Uncle's, Aunt's, and probably Dog's Days. All needing a card, all needing a present. Someone, please, say 'Enough!'.

East meets west

The delightful habits of some Asian countries are coming to our shores. Small, carefully and tastefully wrapped presents for all kinds of informal occasions – and sometimes for no occasion at all – are the fashion among young people everywhere now. A wonderful fashion it is, too.

a   Which article is critical of present and card giving?
b   Do you enjoy giving cards and presents? Do you like receiving them?
c   Should we give and receive presents more frequently than we do?

Making notes

11   Read this Speaking Part 2 taskcard and the notes made by two candidates. Which set of notes is more practical? Why?

Describe a present you received and that you liked very much.

You should say

who gave it to you and on what occasion

what it was like

what you did with it

and explain why you liked it.

Candidate 1
1 *mother, birthday*
2 *Rulex Explorer Seamaster III*
   gold, blue face, roman numerals
   automatic, date, alarm, time zones
   waterproof, shockproof
3 *wore it, checked the time all the time*
4 *expensive, quality*

Candidate 2
mother, bday
watch, watch features
wore, checked
£ £ £, qual

12   Take one minute to think and make notes about your own talk on this topic, using your own experience. Then practise speaking for two minutes using your notes.

Exam listening

Section 4

 2.16

Questions 31–38

Complete the notes below.
*Write **NO MORE THAN THREE WORDS AND/OR A NUMBER** for each answer.*

The European Starling

Length	12 inches
Colour	**31** .... , white spots.
Nesting sites	**32** ....
Diet	**33** ....
Natural range	British Isles, Finland
Population	British Isles, Finland: in decline
	USA: **34** ....

Some of the problems created by large numbers of starlings

On wildlife

They compete with other species for **35** .... places.

On agriculture

They feed on **36** ....

They cause **37** .... damage.

On human life

They may cause **38** ....

Questions 39 and 40

*Choose the correct letter **A**, **B**, or **C**.*

39 What is regulated by legislation on species movements?

    A   the movement of foreigners

    B   the deposit and pick-up of water

    C   the import and export of fish

40 What is the ultimate deciding factor in species management?

    A   economics

    B   ethics

    C   politics

Health

Topic talk

1 Look at the photos and answer questions a–d below.

a   Which of these sports would you like to play? Which would you prefer to watch?
b   Which of these sports are most and least beneficial to your health?
c   Which sports are the most popular in your country? Why?
d   Which categories below do the sports in the photos belong to? Think of other sports for each category.

water sports	adventure sports	motor sport	blood sports
team sports	non-contact sports	racket sports	indoor sports
	outdoor sports		

2 Match each statement 1–6 with the correct explanation a–f.

1   I prefer contact sports like football and rugby,
2   Swimming is the only individual sport I like,
3   Everyone should take up some form of physical exercise,
4   I like skiing and other winter sports,
5   I suppose I'm mostly interested in spectator sports,
6   The kinds of sports I'm really against are blood sports,

a   since it will keep them healthy and prevent illness.
b   basically because I'm not a very energetic person.
c   just because I don't believe people should take pleasure in that sort of thing.
d   not least because they're a good way to get rid of my aggression.
e   but they're obviously difficult to do all year round.
f   as I usually prefer being with other people.

3 With a partner, ask and answer these questions. Give reasons for your answers.

   a   What is your favourite sport?
   b   Which areas of sport appeal to you?
   c   Which areas of sport would you avoid?

4 Decide which two words in the list cannot follow the word *sports*.

> event   opponent   centre   club   field   opportunity   venue
> coverage   equipment   channel

5 The statements below were made by people who enjoy sport. Make a list of the benefits of sport that are mentioned in the sentences. Try to express them in general not personal terms. Which three statements do you think are the most important?

   a   Doing sport has made me more mentally alert.
   b   Since I've been doing more exercise, I get fewer illnesses.
   c   One thing that's important is that I'm still learning new skills.
   d   Part of the reason I play football is to meet new people.
   e   After doing some exercise, I always feel more relaxed.
   f   Something you have to learn is how to be part of a team.
   g   The main reason I take part is because there's a competitive atmosphere.
   h   I was partly attracted to do more sport by the opportunity to be outdoors.

6 In Speaking Part 3, you will be asked to respond to some more abstract questions. Match the benefits you identified in 5 with the questions below.

   a   What do you think is the link between sport and a healthy population?
   b   What do you think is the cause of the increase in people doing sport?
   c   How important is the social aspect of participating in sport?

7 With a partner, ask and answer the questions in 6. Give more detailed examples, using the phrases in 5 and the trigger words below to help you.

> if … , then   for example   so that   as   because   since

1 The list below contains some problems which students often encounter at university. Number them from 1–6 according to how serious you think they are (1 = most serious; 6 = least serious).

feeling homesick

examination pressure

colds and flu

poor accommodation

language difficulties

student debt

2 Answer questions a–c below.

a Which other problems can new students encounter?

b Look at the table in 3 below. Which of the student services listed could help with the problems in 1?

c If you experienced problems at university, who would you go to for help?

3 The table below comes from a table completion task. Answer questions a–c.

a What do the numbers tell you about the order in which you will hear the information?

b Which of the missing spaces are likely to be numbers? What kind of numbers?

c What can you predict for the other gaps?

Staying healthy at Glenfield

Student services	Location	Cost	Availability
Health centre	North Campus	Example: ...£6.50... charge for prescriptions	All students within the 1 .... zone
Counselling service	North Campus	Up to **2** .... consultations free	All students
Nightline	**3** .... Campus	Free	By phone: call **4** ....
Sports centre	South Campus	**5** .... each year	All students

4 2.17 Listen to the recording and complete the table. Write NO MORE THAN TWO WORDS AND/OR A NUMBER for each answer.

Words spelt out

5 Some letters in the English alphabet sound alike. For example *p* rhymes with *g*, and *a* rhymes with *j*. Complete the lists below with the remaining letters of the alphabet in English.

a b c d e f g h i j k l m n o p q r s t u v w x y z

List 1:	a,
List 2:	b,
List 3:	f,
List 4:	i,
List 5	q,
List 6	r, o, w, z (None of these rhymes with any other letters.)

6 2.18 Listen to the lists in 5 and check your answers.

7 2.19 Listen to a person leaving a message on an answering machine. Complete the form below.

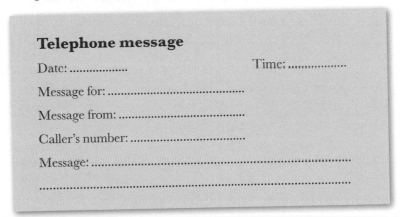

Telephone message

Date: ....   Time: ....

Message for: ....

Message from: ....

Caller's number: ....

Message: ....

....

8 Make notes for a telephone message of your own. With a partner, leave a message. Where necessary, spell out words.

9 2.20 Listen to the second part of the recording, which follows on from the table completion task in 3. Complete the form below. Write NO MORE THAN THREE WORDS AND/OR A NUMBER for each answer.

Material request form

Documents requested:	**6** ....
Student name:	**7** ....
Address:	22 **8** ....
	Glenfield
Postcode:	**9** 9BQ
Nationality:	Swiss
Age:	24
Course:	**10** ....

Technique

Prepare for form-filling by familiarizing yourself with the sounds in the English alphabet.

1   Read the ten ideas below on how to improve your health, and answer questions a–c.

   a   How many of the ideas do you personally apply in your life?
   b   Are there any ideas which you do not agree with?
   c   Are there any other causes of poor health that the advice does not cover?

Ten easy ways to improve your health

   1   Apply sun cream when outdoors on sunny days.

   2   Eat at least five portions of fruit and vegetables each day.

   3   Stop smoking.

   4   Avoid high-fat convenience foods.

   5   Control how much salt and sugar you eat.

   6   Drink at least 1.5 litres of water each day.

   7   Start a holistic form of exercise, like yoga or *tai chi*.

   8   Take vitamin supplement tablets each day.

   9   Avoid stress by balancing work and play.

   10 Do thirty minutes of moderate exercise on most days.

2   In Speaking Part 3 you will be asked some abstract questions about a topic. It is important to be able to understand exactly what the examiner asks so that you can answer appropriately. Which questions below would have basically the same information in the answer?

Example

a is similar to *g*

   a   In what ways is the modern diet better or worse that the diet of the past?
   b   What are the main causes of ill-health in the modern world?
   c   How can people take steps to improve their general level of health?
   d   In what ways are sport and health linked?
   e   Which factors are contributing to low levels of health in the world today?
   f   Are sport and health connected? If so, how?
   g   How is the food we eat different from the food eaten by previous generations?
   h   To what extent can alternative approaches to medicine have a positive effect?
   i   How effective is alternative medicine in helping people improve their health?
   j   What are the most effective ways of getting and staying healthy?

3   Which ideas in 1 are relevant to each question in 2?

Emphasizing main points

4   2.21 Listen to three speakers answering questions from 2. Match each speaker with the correct question.

Speaker 1: ....
Speaker 2: ....
Speaker 3: ....

5   2.21 The list below gives some phrases for emphasizing your main points. Listen again to the three speakers. Match each phrase with the correct speaker.

It's mostly because of …
I suppose the best way is …
The main cause seems to be …
I'd say … is the key thing.
I think the most effective way is …
It's obvious that …

Taking time to think

6   The comments in a–c below were made to students preparing for Speaking Part 3. Which statement gives an accurate reflection of the test?

a   If you do not have a clear answer for every topic presented, you will get a bad mark.
b   If you do not have a clear answer to an unexpected question, you can admit this and give the best answer that you can.
c   If you do not have a clear answer to an unexpected question, you should tell the examiner and ask to move on to the next question.

Technique

Some questions may be difficult and unexpected. Take a moment to think up your answer if necessary. Explaining that you are unsure can give you time to think.

7   2.21 Each speaker in the recording used a phrase to delay giving their answer. Listen again and write the phrases below.

Speaker 1: ....
Speaker 2: ....
Speaker 3: ....

8   With a partner, ask and answer the questions in 2. Use the phrases for taking time to think and for emphasizing main points to help you express your own ideas. Give reason for your answers.

9 Read the two short articles below and answer the questions.

    a   In what ways do they disagree with the health advice we normally receive?

    b   How would these articles change your answers to the questions you discussed in 8?

Are you an exercise addict?

An occasional trip to the gym is fine, but increasing numbers of people find that exercise becomes the main organizing principle for each day. In extreme cases, some individuals have found that their exercise regime affects their job and their relationships. With the trend towards 'healthy' living, this is set to become an even bigger problem in the future.

An egg a day keeps the doctor away

Only a few years ago, we were being warned that there was so much cholesterol in eggs that we shouldn't eat more than two or three a week. Now, nutritionists have changed their minds: eggs are no longer a danger food, and the cholesterol they contain has little or no effect on our health. This just goes to show that our concerns about diet might be misplaced.

10 With a partner, ask and answer the questions below.

    a   How is good health related to education and wealth?

    b   What dangers are associated with exercise and sport?

    c   To what extent is healthy food compatible with enjoyable food?

Pronunciation: contrastive stress

11 Indicate the stress on each sentence so that they give the emphasis indicated in the brackets. The first one is done for you.

    a   Put on <u>sun</u>-cream before you go out. (remember to use sun-cream)
         Put on sun-cream be<u>fore</u> you go out. (don't wait until after you have gone out)

    b   Thirty minutes daily is a good amount of exercise. (not sixty)
         Thirty minutes daily is a good amount of exercise. (not weekly)

    c   Fresh fruit is good for everyone. (not just for children)
         Fresh fruit is good for everyone. (not frozen or canned fruit)

    d   Fish is good for the brains of children. (it really is true!)
         Fish is good for the brains of children. (children not adults)

12   2.22 Listen to the recording and check.

13 Correct the following facts about health in the UK.

    a   Men spend thirty minutes a week on sport. (day)

    b   Men spend fifteen minutes a day on sport. (women)

    c   The life expectancy of women is seventy-seven years. (men)

    d   The life expectancy of women is eighty-eight years. (eighty-one)

Exam listening

Section 2

 2.23

Questions 11–15

Label the plan below.
*Write **NO MORE THAN TWO WORDS** for each answer.*

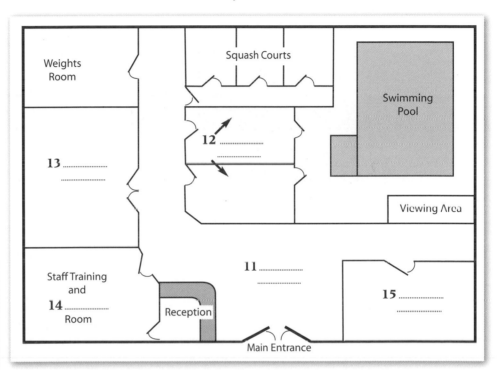

 2.24

Questions 16–20

Complete the table below.
*Write **NO MORE THAN THREE WORDS AND/OR A NUMBER** for each answer.*

Membership type	Cost	Access	Additional benefits
Anytime	**16**	Any time between 5 a.m. and midnight	Access to **17** .... clubs nationwide.
Freetime	£500	Between 10 a.m. and 3 p.m.	Access to **18** ....
Standard	£400	Same as Freetime, but only **19**	None
Children	**20** .... discount	Depends on choice of scheme	Depends on choice of scheme

Individual and society

Topic talk

1 Look at the photo below and answer questions a–c.

   a How would you feel about being part
      of a crowd like this?
   b Do you think individuals shape
      society or is it the other way round?
      Why?
   c In what ways can people have a
      positive influence on the society they
      live in?

2 Complete sentences a–h below by adding an appropriate word from the list.
      The first one has been done for you.

> issue   initiatives   difficulty   attitudes   aspect   area   outline
> alternative

   a Let's now examine the range of *initiatives* the government has introduced
      to promote social awareness.
   b Another major .... that we face here is the quality of research.
   c One .... of the problem that has yet to be considered is the cost to
      society.
   d Another problem .... we must examine is the meaning of the word
      society.
   e Let us now look at the burning .... of individual responsibility.
   f Let's start with a brief .... of the course.
   g One obvious .... to consider was closing the project down.
   h First, let us consider the various .... people hold towards enterprise in
      society.

3 When you listen to a talk, you need to be able to follow the guidance given
      by the speaker. Decide the function of each of the sentences a–h above.
      Choose from the functions in 1–3 below.

   Example

   a   *3*

   1   the very beginning of a talk
   2   part of a sequence of points
   3   beginning a new sequence of points

4 Replace the words in the sentences in 2 with words from the list below. In some cases, more than one word will be possible.

> question   sketch   summary   problem   viewpoints   hurdle
> proposals   obstacle   facet   plans

5 The extract below comes from a lecturer's talk. Decide which words in the extract can be replaced by the items a–g.

a   topics   e   concerns
b   influence   f   requirement
c   effect   g   need
d   theories

> In today's session, we are going to examine the latest thinking regarding the necessity for societies in the world to foster international cooperation on a wide range of issues. We are going to look into the dynamics of collaboration at a society level first and then see if individual organizations or indeed individuals can have any impact. So, let us now go through this list of problems on the first slide.

6 Match at least one solution from the list below to each international problem a–g.

> flood prevention   trade and political partnerships
> investing strategically in job creation   sharing information and technology
> international water preservation programme
> sharing ideas on how to cope with changes
> research into management of assets

a   Water shortages are a major cause for concern.
b   Some countries are too small to be heard on the international stage.
c   Poverty is increasing not declining.
d   Flooding is causing serious damage in both rich and poor countries.
e   Demographic changes are affecting the balance within societies.
f   Natural resources are becoming exhausted.
g   Some countries are being left behind while other countries are advancing rapidly.

7 With a partner, practise asking and answering the questions below. Use the ideas in 6 to help you.

a   How do you think individuals can best contribute to society?
b   Do you think modern societies are in danger of being destroyed by materialism?
c   What is the impact of modern business developments worldwide on societies in general?

Listening skills   Paraphrasing questions

1 For each statement below, decide whether it reflects your attitude to life.

   a   I always wear exactly what I like. I don't care if other people think it's not appropriate.
   b   Being on time is really important. It's important to respect others' feelings by not being late.
   c   Is it always wrong to break the law? It depends. For small things it's OK, provided you don't get caught.
   d   I normally do what I'm told at work. Even if I disagree, I keep my head down. It's easier that way.

2 Answer the questions below.

   a   Would you describe yourself as a conformist or a rebel?
   b   Which group makes the biggest contribution to society: conformists or rebels?

Technique

In the test, paraphrasing questions in your head can help you predict the sentences you might hear in the recording.

3 The questions below are taken from a short-answer question task. Read the questions and decide which question sentences a and b relate to.

> 1   Where was Solomon Asch born?
> 2   Which area of interest made Asch take up psychology?
> 3   What was the name of Asch's famous experiment?
> 4   Who were the majority of participants in each experiment?

   a   Asch was attracted to take up psychology because he was interested in ....
   b   It was his interest in .... that made Asch decide to take up psychology.

4 For the other questions in 3, write two gapped sentences that paraphrase the question.

5 2.25 Listen to the first part of the recording. Answer the questions in 3. Write NO MORE THAN THREE WORDS for each answer.

Visual multiple choice

6 Questions 5 and 6 opposite are taken from a visual multiple-choice task. Which pie-chart in 5 is described by the sentence below?

The pie-chart shows that fifteen per cent of people gave the wrong answer, whereas 85 per cent gave the right answer.

7 Write brief sentences describing the pie charts in A and C.

8 Write brief sentences describing the diagrams in Question 6. Choose words from the list below to help you.

equal	vertical	shortest	on the right	in the middle	longest
		on the left	horizontal		

Question 5

Which pie chart shows the proportion of people who gave the incorrect judgement?

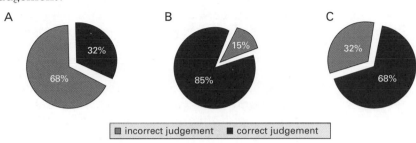

Question 6

Which diagram shows the content of the first card used in the experiment?

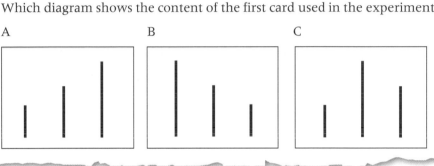

9   2.26 Listen to the recording and answer Questions 5 and 6 above and multiple-choice Questions 7–10 below.

Questions 7 and 8

*Choose TWO letters **A–E**.*

Which two features changed the results of the experiment?

A   a bigger group

B   the number of lines

C   more time

D   gender

E   privacy

Questions 9 and 10

*Choose TWO letters **A–E**.*

Subjects explained their conformity as a desire to

A   keep the experimenter happy.

B   give a good impression.

C   leave early.

D   please the other participants.

E   appear clever.

1   Read the texts below. What kind of place is being described in each text?

> There's something about the place that just feels oppressive. When I've finished what I have to do, I just want to get out as quick as I can. I think it might be because of the fluorescent lighting, which gives me a bit of a headache, and the air-conditioning, which drones on and on. After I've been there all week, staring at those grey walls, I feel emotionally drained. But, that's life.

> It's difficult to describe what really invigorates me, just a freshness that feels good. I always go whenever I feel down about something and need a bit of cheering up. I love the sound of the water, which always relaxes me, and the saltiness on the air. There aren't normally many people around either. It's a bit off the beaten track, so I always manage to get the place more or less to myself.

2   Answer the questions below about places and feelings.

  a   In what ways can places affect our sense of well-being?
  b   How do the places we grow up in affect our character?
  c   What types of place attract you? Which do you avoid?

3   Complete the sentences below with adjectives from the list. What places do you think these are?

dull   busy   deserted   exciting   peaceful   wild   colourful friendly

  a   I like it because it's so .... It's nice to be where there are lots of people.
  b   I suppose it's quite a .... place. There isn't much of interest to do.
  c   Sometimes it's completely .... There's nobody around at all.
  d   With the wind and the weather, and only the birds for company, it's a really .... place.
  e   I love watching the competitive spirit of the two teams. There's a really .... atmosphere in the stadium.
  f   The staff are really helpful, and it's easy to meet new people over a drink. It's a very .... place.
  g   What makes it easy to relax and think is how .... it is. No noises or surprises.
  h   I like the flowers: all bright yellows, reds and blues. It's a very .... experience.

4   Replace each adjective in the sentences in 3 with a near synonym from the list below.

crowded   vibrant   boring   welcoming   quiet   sensuous   empty remote

5 For each category a–e, think of a place where you go in your life to do these things.

    a   a place I go to have fun
    b   a place I go to relax
    c   a place I go to work or study
    d   a place I go to eat
    e   a place I go to be alone

6 With a partner, describe the places you chose using the adjectives. Explain why you chose the adjectives you did.

Starting your description

7 2.27 Listen to three people describing a place which is important to them. Decide which speaker describes the types of places a–c. Make a note of any reasons they give for their choice.

Speaker 1: ....

Speaker 2: ....

Speaker 3: ....

    a   an urban place
    b   a domestic space
    c   a rural area

8 2.27 Listen again and make a note of the expressions that each speaker uses to introduce the place they have chosen.

Speaker 1: ....

Speaker 2: ....

Speaker 3: ....

9 Read the Speaking Part 2 taskcard below. Take one minute to think and make notes about your own talk on this topic, using your own experience. Then practise speaking for two minutes using your notes.

Describe a place which is important to you.

You should say

    where it is

    what activities you normally do there

    what feelings you associate with the place

and explain what influence it has on your life.

Summing up impressions

10 In the last part of the Speaking Part 2 taskcard, you are normally asked to sum up your personal impressions. Match each mini taskcard 1–3 with the phrases a–g that you could use to answer it.

> 1 Describe a place where you spent a memorable holiday … and explain why you particularly liked or disliked this place.
>
> 2 Describe an experience in which you tried something new … and explain how this experience has influenced you.
>
> 3 Describe something special that you bought … and explain why this item is special to you.

a I particularly liked/disliked this … because …

b Its main effect on me has been …

c I feel attached to this … because …

d The main reason for my reaction was …

e What I've learnt from this is …

f The influence this has had on me is …

g This taught me an important lesson: …

11 Think of your answer to each of the mini taskcards in 9. With a partner, give your answers, using the phrases above.

Pronunciation: past simple endings

12 2.28 In each sentence, write /t/ or /d/ or /ɪd/ next to the verbs, according to the pronunciation of the simple past tense. One has been done for you. Listen to the recording to check.

a I tried (............) a parachuting course last year.
b I liked (............) it a lot.
c I almost panicked (............) in the plane.
d But I jumped (/t/).
e I landed (............) very softly – thank goodness.

13 Complete the short narrative using the simple past of the verbs in brackets. Write the pronunciation of the ending after each verb eg /t/, /d/, or /ɪd/.

We **1** .... (start) our walk at 2 p.m. We **2** .... (climb) the cliffs and

3 .... (picnic) on the top. We **4** .... (watch) the sun set and

5 .... (camp) there for the night. Next morning we **6** .... (collect)

our things and **7** .... (start) off again. We **8** .... (arrive) back at

lunchtime and **9** .... (enjoy) a huge lunch at the village pub.

14 Practise saying the narrative, paying special attention to the simple past endings.

Exam listening

Section 3

 2.29

Questions 21–24

Choose the correct letter, **A**, **B**, *or* **C**.

21 Mike is concerned about their assignment because

    A   there is too little time.

    B   it's too difficult.

    C   they have not prepared.

22 What aspect of social welfare does their assignment explore?

    A   a survey of the whole subject

    B   a definition of the main terms

    C   a comparison of different approaches

23 Which approach to the assignment does Fiona recommend?

    A   giving a personal view

    B   taking a balanced approach

    C   agreeing with the tutor

24 How long does the assignment have to be?

    A   at least 2,000 words

    B   at least 3,000 words

    C   at least 4,000 words

2.30

Questions 25 and 26

Complete the sentences below.
Write **NO MORE THAN THREE WORDS AND/OR A NUMBER** *for each answer.*

Professor Green's lecture is called **25** ....

It takes place in the Becket building at 10 a.m. on **26** ....

Questions 27–30

Complete the table below.
Write **NO MORE THAN TWO WORDS AND/OR A NUMBER** *for each answer.*

Title	Author	Publisher	Year
27	**28**	Glenfield University Press	2006
29 .... in Britain	Edward Jones	Rutland University Press	**30** ....

Unit 1

Topic talk

1

a Students' own answer.
b Possible answer
Students can be given grants by the government or they can be given vouchers to help subsidize their rent.
c Students' own answer.

2

a penthouse
b house
c studio
d farmhouse
e bungalow
f terraced house
g shared house

3

1 a   3 c
2 d   4 g

4

a fascinating
b cramped
c modern
d bustling
e uncomfortable
f shabby
g boring

5

Students' own answer.

6

1 c   4 a
2 e   5 b
3 d

7

1 e   4 c
2 b   5 a
3 d

8

Reason   because/with
Consequence   so

9

Students' own answers.

Listening skills

1

1 c   3 b
2 a

2

1 good
2 terraced house
3 £125,000
4 18.2°
5 612 mm
6 3,567
7 £2.20
8 75%/25%
9 25%/75%

3

Tables 1 and 2 are read from left to right.
Table 3 is read from top to bottom.

4

a analogue and digital radios
b two
c five
d 1, 4

5

a must be wrong: three words
c must be wrong: two numbers
d must be wrong: two words are acceptable, but two numbers are not.

6

1 £95
2 stations
3 (sound) quality
4 1 year/one year
5 battery life

Script

Customer I'm interested in buying a radio. Can you help me?
Assistant Yes, of course. As you can see, we have this analogue radio on special offer today for £29.99. They are normally £35. We've also got a much more modern range of digital radios – these are over here.
Customer Oh yes? What are they?
Assistant They're the new technology. This one, for example, sells at £95. The analogue radios are looking a bit old-fashioned now.
Customer Are they? What's so good about these new ones?
Assistant Well, the main advantage with the analogue ones is, of course, cheapness, but the main advantage with the digital ones is the number and variety of *stations* you can get – hundreds of them. All kinds of stations, playing music – rock, pop, classical, everything in fact, as well as news, current affairs, comedy … all sorts.
Customer What about the sound quality?
Assistant The quality is very good. Under certain circumstances, you can get amazing *sound quality* with analogue, but this is usually with very expensive radios which would normally be part of a hi-fi sound system – we have lots of those on the third floor if you're interested. The second great thing about digital is clarity: you get no interference, well, less interference than with analogue. You get a very clear and clean sound.
Customer Well, I want a radio for the flat I share with three other friends of mine.
Assistant Well, you want something that will last. The analogues come with a *one-year*

guarantee but the digitals have a two-year guarantee which is extendable to three years if you pay an extra £26. The main disadvantage with analogue is that it will be turned off in a few years – we don't know exactly when, but sometime.

Customer But what about the batteries – I've heard that they use a lot of batteries.

Assistant That probably is the one disadvantage of the digital radios. The *battery life* is not very long, but they all come with rechargeable batteries, which really solves the problem.

7

a The numbers suggest that the speakers will discuss each category on the left in turn.

b All missing information appears numerical. The SuperValue card will perhaps be better than the old ValueCard, so you may be able to predict that numbers will be within a certain range.

8

6	3/three	9	20/twenty
7	22.5	10	12
8	1/one		

Script

Assistant So, how would you like to pay?

Customer Er, cash.

Assistant I wondered if you had a Robson's Store Card.

Customer Do you know, I think I do. Here we are.

Assistant Oh my goodness, I haven't seen one of those for a long time. Those are the old ValueCards. Now you can get a SuperValue Card which is even better value.

Customer Really? I don't know what to do.

Assistant Well, I can change you onto a SuperValue Card if you want. With the SuperValue Card you get double the standard

number of points, and your free credit period is longer. With your old card you get one month's free credit, but you can get *three months'* free credit with the new card. The interest rate is a bit higher, at *22.5 per cent* rather than 18.5 per cent, but if you're careful you don't have to pay interest at all.

Customer Well, I'm not sure about that – it seems better in some ways. Can I continue to use my old card?

Assistant You certainly can, until they withdraw them, which I'm sure they will before too long. But with the SuperValue Card there are special cardholder-only days – two per month, compared with *one* per month with the old card.

Customer I see. My old card gave me free delivery, too.

Assistant That's right, free delivery within *twenty* miles. The SuperValue Card gives you free delivery up to 50 miles.

Customer That sounds good. I think the old card was free, too.

Assistant With the SuperValue there is an initial fee of just *£12*, and then it's very good value.

Customer I think I'll pay cash.

Assistant Very good, madam.

Speaking skills

1

Script

a Can you tell me your full name?

b And what shall I call you?

c Where do you come from?

d Could you show me your ID?

2

Candidate Hallo, good *afternoon*.

Examiner Good *afternoon*. Can you *tell* me your *full* name, please?

Candidate My name is *Benjamin Weiss*.

Examiner And what can I *call* you?

Candidate Please *call* me *Ben*.

Examiner Good. Where *do* you come *from*?

Candidate I come *from Switzerland*.

Examiner Can you *show* me your identification, please?

Candidate Of course. *Here* is my *passport*.

3

Students' own answers.

4

1	f	5	b
2	c	6	h
3	g	7	a
4	d	8	e

5

a They relate to personal information.

b Answers a, d, f, g, and h are especially good.
In a and f, there is a short answer followed by a further (short) description.
In g and h, there is a direct answer followed by an explanation.
In d, a direct answer is followed by further relevant information.

6

Students' own answers.

7

Students' own answers.

8

1 Could you tell me something about where you live?

2 What sort of place is that?

3 Is there anything you particularly like about it?

4 And what kind of jobs do people do there?

Script

Examiner Now in this first part I'd like to ask you some questions about yourself. Let's talk about your town or village.

Candidate OK.

Examiner Could you tell me something about where you live?

Candidate Yes. I used to live in Switzerland but I've recently moved to the UK. Now I live in Weybridge.

Examiner What sort of place is that?

Candidate It's a large, busy place. It's near London. It has got lots and lots of people and houses – it's typical of a London suburb.

Examiner Is there anything you particularly like about it?

Candidate The great thing about Weybridge is the facilities. You've got everything you need: shops, buses and trains, cinemas, pubs and restaurants, entertainment. It's never necessary to leave it! You've got all you want!

Examiner I see. And what kind of jobs do people do there?

Candidate All kinds. I suppose mostly people work in offices, for big companies. Some people work in shops. There are a lot of hi-tech companies around there.

Examiner Thank you. Now let's talk about what you do …

9

1 moved here from Switzerland recently
2 large, busy place, near London – lots of people
3 the facilities – he gives a list of them
4 offices, companies, shops, hi-tech companies.
   In questions 1 and 2, the candidate gives extra information.
   In answer to questions 3 and 4, the candidate gives a short answer and then gives examples.

10

Students' own answers.

11

Students' own answers.

12

pleasant	2	cramped	1
dynamic	3	bungalow	3
flat	1	detached	2
peaceful	2	overpriced	3

13

Pattern 1	flat, cramped
Pattern 2	pleasant, peaceful
Pattern 3	detached
Pattern 4	bungalow
Pattern 5	dynamic
Pattern 6	overpriced

14

a also: pattern 2, not 3
b offend: pattern 3, not 2
c example: pattern 5, not 4
d certainly: pattern 4, not 5
e open: pattern 2, not 3
f unpleasant: pattern 5, not 4
g cancel: pattern 2, not 3

Exam listening

Questions 11–15

11 full-time students
12 part-time students
13 distance learners
14 make an appointment
15 (your) ID card

Script

Librarian Good morning. My name is Mandy and I am going to tell you a little about the John R Jones Memorial Library here at Blackwater College. We regard the library as a gateway to the resources that you as students at the college may need. The majority of you are *full-time students* – you may find you spend a lot of time here. Even those of you who are *part-time students* will no doubt require the services too. I hope that by the end of this short talk you will know the services the library has to offer, including the website, and how to get any further help you may need. Sorry, I forgot there may be a few *distance learners* on the tour today. I'll explain about the online facilities and borrowing by post scheme a little later on. This is the main site of the library, but we also have the Rivergate building and the Fieldhouse Library. The Rivergate building houses the Geography resources, that is the book collection and the journal collection as well as the map collection. The hours and days of opening of the Rivergate collection are the same as this building except that it is closed on Christmas Day and New Year's Day. The Fieldhouse Library contains a specialist collection of local history and if you want to visit it you will need to *make an appointment*. Those two facilities are the only exceptions to the rule that all the Blackwater College libraries are open 24 hours a day, seven days a week, 365 days a year. However, to gain access to the facilities you must have *your ID card* – no ID card, no entry. We have heard all the stories and excuses and we don't accept any of them. Just remember your ID card!

Questions 16–20

16 Economics
17 French Literature
18 the new restaurant
19 150
20 national newspapers

Script

Librarian Now I must apologize for the mess you can see around you today. Libraries should be quiet places, but unfortunately this is not currently the case here. This new building has been here for only two months, and as a result we have not quite finished moving in! So far, we have moved most of the book and journal collections from the old library into this new building. There are two exceptions: we are currently moving the *Economics* collection here, which should be installed by tomorrow, and we will be moving the *French Literature* collection into this building next week. But, as you can see, we are still building *the new restaurant*. We will finish it, we hope, very shortly. We have finished the cafe, however, and students can use it during the library opening hours. We have recently installed *150* computer places and we will be adding another 100 shortly, so that there will be plenty for everybody very soon. Very shortly this library will be one of the finest in this part of the country. Don't forget that the library isn't just about academic books. In addition to the books and journals there is a wide range of *national newspapers* available from the librarians on request. I'd like to mention the different ways you can get help in using our resources. Don't forget our website at www.mlbc.ac.uk. There are the full catalogues, and journal access is available if you have your password and ID number. Now, any questions?

Unit 2

Topic talk

1

Possible answers

a   The train ticket probably reminds the speaker of a memorable journey.
   The music notes perhaps trigger memories of a special event or person.
   The postcard probably reminds the speaker of a special person.
b   The memories are happy, because of the adjective *unforgettable*.
c   Students' own answer.

2

a   marvellous great
b   happy remarkable
c   great momentous
d   memorable favourable
e   exhilarating rewarding
f   exciting big
g   outstanding impressive
h   golden happy
i   fantastic great

3

Possible answers

thoroughly: *exciting*, memorable, impressive
highly: rewarding, exciting
very: happy, exhilarating, rewarding, big, impressive, favourable
totally: happy, exhilarating, rewarding, outstanding

4

a   an experience
b   an achievement
c   an event
d   a special occasion
e   an adventure

5

Possible answers

an achievement: I came first in the school swimming gala.
an event: I went to an open-air pop concert.
an occasion: I attended my sister's twenty-first birthday party.
an experience: I worked for several months in a bank.
an adventure: I travelled around Europe on my own.

6

Students' own answers.

7

a   rewarding experience
b   unforgettable moment
c   bizarre incident
d   memorable trip
e   formal occasion
f   nerve-racking adventure
g   exhilarating experience
h   humbling experience

Listening skills

1

Starting: e, h
Listing: c, f, h
Adding: a, i
Digressing: d
Returning to the subject: b
Concluding: c, g

2

b	g
e	c
d	f
a	

3

a	false	d	false
b	true	e	true
c	true	f	true

5

1	2/two	3	exciting
2	economics		

Script

Lecturer Good morning, everybody. I'd like to begin this term's lectures with a discussion of the various sub-disciplines in history. Before I do that though, can I refer you to the handout you picked up on the way in? It deals with *two* general topics. The first is 'Why study history?' and the second is 'What is history?'. Neither of these questions has an easy answer. In fact, people have been asking these questions for as long as history has been studied. However, as you are mostly new students to this subject – and we have some students of *economics* with us also – I feel you should have some background to these basic questions. Anyway it's all in the handout. I might add that for me personally, the most important reason for studying history is that I find it *exciting*. Our ancestors can remain, if we want them to, a mystery, a closed book, a blackness that we never see into. Or, we can come to know what motivated them and discover how that led to the world we live in today.

6

1	B	4	C
2	B	5	B
3	A	6	B

7

The exact dates, or expressions such as *the eighteen hundreds*.

8

Possible answer

You can predict that *post-modern history* does not sound *traditional*; *political history* and *military history* sound traditional; and *feminist history* sounds modern. You expect to hear expressions such as: *old-fashioned, familiar, conventional, current, up-to-date, contemporary, progressive, forward-looking, modern,* and *new.*

9

4	T	8	M
5	F	9	T
6	F	10	M
7	M		

Script

Lecturer You who have chosen to pursue the study of history are very fortunate. This is a time when we can talk not just about history but histories. Traditionally, history was seen as one subject and the subject matter was clear. It was about kings and queens and wars. Additionally, it was about states and empires or groups of states. This is what we now call political history. The sub-topics were the parts of the world – for example, the history of China or of France. History has moved on somewhat, and we can learn a lot about current views of history by looking at the proposed lecture topics in our leading universities. In fact, you'll see that even the

simplest definition of history – that it is about what happened in the past – is up for grabs. Some of the more, how shall I put it, progressive areas of study are as much about what should happen in the future. One example of this is the field of post-modern history. Likewise, feminist history looks at the past to make sure the future will be different, and it uses the past to assist in its efforts to make the future as it wants it to be. Somewhere in the middle of these two extremes lie a range of areas of study which have developed over the modern period, replacing the traditional idea of political history. These are by now mostly well established. You can study social history or economic history. Social history asks about the ordinary people and their lives. Not just their daily lives but their contribution to changes in our society. Ordinary people have desires and wishes which they try to put into effect and this has a massive effect on social development which was not fully understood in the traditional study of history. By the way, one area of traditional history which I forgot to mention, but which has had a resurgence of interest in recent years, is the area of military history. This was, of course, of great practical use in more violent times and unfortunately has become of increasing use and interest – academically and practically – in our own times. By the way, there is a new series of lectures on military history in our department – as if to demonstrate the truth of what I have just said. Ethnic and multi-cultural history are further examples of kinds of history which, like social history, differ from the traditional forms. Ethnic history is a modern concern which concentrates on the value systems and beliefs of a people – usually a minority people – which were ignored in the rapid forward march of the

rich and powerful nations and states. How various ethnic groups live together and how their traditions change and develop is the subject of its contemporary cousin multi-cultural history. In sum, as I said, you are fortunate to have such a wide choice of things to study in the fields of history. Choose wisely. And finally, it only remains for me to wish you good luck in your studies.

Speaking skills

1

Possible answers

a Found – in a shop window, perhaps
   Lost – in a newspaper, shop window

b The purse owner may find the purse, with or without the cards, especially if she has lost it near the shop, and sees the notice. The wallet owner may be less lucky. The finder may not want the trouble of phoning.

c 30 per cent as a reward seems reasonable. However, £10 is not a lot of money, so maybe a finder will keep the wallet, rather than claim the reward.

d Students' own answer.

2

Students' own answers.

3

He lost his car. It was very important to him – a precious, beautiful, wonderful thing.

Script

I should say, and, yes, this is something I forgot to say, this car was the most precious, beautiful, wonderful thing in my life at that time. And there I was. Without it. I'd lost it. I felt very … how shall I put it? … stupid. Now, where was I? Oh yes, talking to the policeman. He didn't really take any notice of me. He didn't laugh, but he did look very uninterested. Now next, … let me see … yes, the next thing that happened was that …

4

a	3	c	1
b	4	d	2

5

a   losing an important thing

b   six

c   one refers to the future; five refer to the past

6

Possible answers

1   what efforts you made to find it

2   what efforts you made to find it

3   what you will do in the future

4   describing the important thing

5   why the thing was important to you

6   what efforts you made to find it

7   how you lost it

7

Possible answer

I remember one time when I lost a handbag. Well, I should say first that it was probably my own fault. Looking back, I realize I had a habit of putting it down. I think I lost it in a shop. It had all my cards in it, so I was desperate. Anyway, to find it, I first went back to the shop, but they couldn't help. After that, I went to the police. They suggested I put an ad in the newspaper, so finally, that's what I did. In future, I won't use a handbag. I'll always use a bag with a shoulder strap.

8

Students' own answers.

9

in case

10

a   In future, I will put some keys in a flower pot in the front garden in case I lose my house keys.

b   In future, I will keep a note of my password in case I can't get into my emails.

c   In future, I will note the number of my embassy in case I lose my passport.

d   In future, I will keep a second umbrella in the car in case I leave mine at home.

e   In future, I will keep a twenty-pound note in my shoe in case somebody robs me in the street.

f   In future, I will write down the phone number of my bank in case I lose my credit card.

11

Students' own answers.

12

a	can	c	can
b	can't	d	can't

Script

a   I can remember my favourite childhood toy.

b   I can't remember my first holiday.

c   I can recall a time when I got lost.

d   My first day at school was a day I can't forget.

13

Students' own answers.

14

Students' own answers.

Exam listening

Questions 21–25

21   costs and benefits

22   small

23   raise money

24   (about) 100

25   (display) cabinets

Script

Anne   Hello Tom!

Tom   Hello Anne!

Anne   What have you been doing?

Tom   Oh, just sitting around, catching up with some reading.

Anne   I've had a great time. You know we're doing this assignment on, what is it?

Tom   'Museums – their *costs and benefits*.'

Anne   That's right. Well, I've been to the Sandgate Museum. It was really good. These local museums are really interesting because they connect people with the history of one special place. We all know about kings and emperors and battles and wars, but local museums tell us about the everyday lives of ordinary people and that's why they are so important.

Tom   I'm not so sure about that. I think they are of interest but they're so small that they can't give a true picture. They do their best.

Anne   I don't really agree. They do give a true picture, but perhaps not a full picture. It's the truth but not the whole truth.

Tom   I think the smallness is the number one problem. Because they're *small* and local they attract few visitors. That's why they have so little money. And because they have little money they can't buy or maintain many really interesting exhibits. As a result, the shop is almost as big as the museum to try to *raise money* by selling souvenirs, postcards, sweets and so on.

Anne I think they find it difficult, but not impossible. And don't forget, they get a lot of their exhibits free from local people. There was this boat, for example, that was fantastic!

Tom Really? What was that?

Anne There was a massive fishing boat, a real one, *about 100 years old*, and you could walk on it, and get the feeling of what fishing in those days was really like.

Tom Sounds quite good. But I've always found that these kinds of museums are a bit dingy. For example, the *display cabinets* are so dark that you can hardly see the exhibits, and the labels are sometimes difficult to read …

Questions 26–30

26 B	29 C
27 C	30 B
28 A	

Script

Anne So coming back to our assignment. What we've got to decide is whether these museums should be funded by the government or just by local people.

Tom I think it depends entirely on what kind of museum it is.

Anne How do you mean?

Tom Well, take local history museums. They are small so they won't survive without financial support. But that should come from the local authority, since only people in that area or tourists will visit it.

Anne I agree, but what about big natural history museums? Surely they should get money from the central government.

Tom Why? Children who want to learn about nature can go out into the countryside with their schoolteachers. They could survive from donations, and they get loads of visitors anyway. The state should spend more on science museums, since not enough people are studying science these days.

Anne I'm not so sure. But I do think a sort of museum which should not get public funds is the craft museum.

Tom Yes, like museums of cotton weaving.

Anne Yeah, which are of interest to only a very small number of people, and they should pay for it.

Tom I agree. But a working farm is a different thing again. That's something from the past of all of us and so it's important to the local community. Kids can learn a lot too. That's the sort of thing that the local government should be spending its money on.

Anne Yes, I agree. Well, I think we've got plenty of ideas for our assignment.

Unit 3

Topic talk

1

Possible answers

a Some people think it isn't, because their card number might not be secure.

b The main effects are that most goods are cheaper. However, such shopping means that certain smaller businesses are closing.

c Students' own answer.

d Students' own answer.

2

A camera doesn't have a lid.

a The lens is scratched.

c The lens cover is missing.

d The zoom lens doesn't work.

3

cloth: cotton, linen, silk
metal: gold, aluminium, brass, tin, steel
man-made: polyester, glass, plastic

4

Possible answers

spherical	globe
rectangular	laptop
square	table top
circular	DVD
oval	plate
spiral	staircase

5

Students' own answer.

6

1	g	5	a
2	b	6	d
3	e	7	h
4	f	8	c

7

a	ripped	f	snapped
b	leaking	g	scratched
c	jammed	h	uncomfortable
d	faded	i	twisted
e	cracked	j	wobbly

8

Possible answers

a You sent me these trousers, and I was really annoyed to find that the trouser leg was completely ripped.

b When I opened the food blender you sent, I found the bowl was leaking very badly.

Listening skills

1

1	c	3	d
2	a	4	b

2

As a result	cause and effect
This means that	cause and effect
If … then	conditional
Firstly	linear ordering
Otherwise	conditional
Next	linear ordering
Unless … , then	conditional
This leads to	cause and effect
Finally,	linear ordering
If not, then	conditional
To begin with,	linear ordering

3

You would expect to hear phrases for linear ordering and conditionals. Phrases for linear ordering could occur at any stage, although *firstly* and *finally* are more restricted to the beginning and end. Phrases for conditionals would occur at question points where two alternatives are available. Phrases for cause and effect are less likely in this flow-chart, but may be common in flowcharts that detail natural processes.

4

a   Start point: customer complains about malfunction End point: customer has working product and is satisfied

b   product repairs, product malfunction, customer complaints

c   *customer, product, error, machine, fill in, fault, repair, form*

d   *firstly, finally, to begin with,* and *next,* since a flowchart describes a sequence of actions; *otherwise, if … then, if not, then,* where there is a question with *yes* or *no* as possible answers.

5

1   repair centre
2   (an) estimate
3   agree
4   collect
5   3/three

Script

Assistant Good morning madam. Can I help you?
Customer Yes, please. I bought this bread making machine from you quite a while ago and it doesn't work.
Assistant I see. That's unusual. These breadmakers are usually very reliable. You didn't over-

fill it, did you? Or put too much water in the mix – those are two reasons for malfunction we often hear of.
Customer No. Certainly not. I had it working for quite a while and then it stopped working. It doesn't do anything now.
Assistant I see. That sounds like a fault in the machine.
Customer Yes. I wonder if you can do anything about it for me.
Assistant Well, that depends. If it is inside the guarantee period we can help you. Otherwise, it will be more difficult.
Customer Let me see. I have the receipt here. I bought it in – it was some time ago – the receipt says, … in February last year.
Assistant February. Well, unfortunately that means it is outside the warranty period. In that case, I'll get you a form which you can fill in and we'll see what we can do.
Customer Well, what can you do, do you think?
Assistant Well, as I say, if you fill in this form, we can send away the breadmaker to be mended. It goes off to a *repair centre*.
Customer Oh good. What happens then?
Assistant Then, we don't get an exact costing, but we will get back an *estimate* of how much it will cost and how long it will take.
Customer I see. And do you think it will be expensive?
Assistant Well, it won't be cheap. There will be labour and parts to think about and also the postage and packing costs.
Customer And we don't know how much they will be?
Assistant Not yet. But when you get the estimate, you've got two options, obviously. If you agree, you can go ahead. Or if you don't, you can say, 'No, it's too expensive'. It's your decision entirely whether you *agree*.
Customer And if I go ahead?

Assistant Then we arrange the repair. We don't have much stock room, so when it is done what we'll have to do is arrange a time for you to *collect* it from us.
Customer All right, that's what I'll do.
Assistant Just give me the receipt.
Customer Here you are.
Assistant Just a minute, madam. I thought you said you bought the breadmaker in February.
Customer That's right. Here is the date. Two – twelve – oh six.
Assistant I think there's some mistake. In the UK, two twelve oh six is the second of December 2006.
Customer Oh, of course. How stupid of me! Of course it is!
Assistant So it's inside the warranty period.
Customer Oh great.
Assistant That's right. That's much easier.
Customer So, what can you do now?
Assistant Very simple. You fill in this form, we replace the machine and return it to your home address within *three* days.
Customer Well, that's excellent.

6

6   217980345
7   Yonge
8   15
9   Capercaillie
10   Monday

Script

Assistant Now, let me have your details.
Customer Certainly.
Assistant Now – this is a Gleeware … Breadmaker 3 … model number?
Customer I have it here – *two – one – seven …*
Assistant Two – one – seven …
Customer *nine – eight – zero …*
Assistant nine – eight –oh
Customer *three – four – five.*

Assistant Thank you. Now, where did you buy it – was it here?

Customer No, it was in your shop in Bluewater.

Assistant I see … Bluewater. Now – date bought – two – twelve – oh six. Now can I have your name?

Customer Yes. It's Yonge, J H Yonge.

Assistant That's …

Customer That's spelt *Y-O-N-G-E*, that's Yonge.

Assistant I see. And your address?

Customer *15* Capercaillie Gardens, Aberdeen.

Assistant Er, I *should* know this, can you tell me …

Customer Yes, it's *C-A-P-E-R* then *C-A-I-double-L-I-E*.

Assistant Sorry, could you say that again?

Customer Sure. C-A-P-E-R-C-A-I-double-L-I-E.

Assistant And Gardens as in Gardens.

Customer Yes.

Assistant Good. And the postcode?

Customer AD22 4SC

Assistant Thank you. And what would be a convenient time of day to deliver the replacement breadmaker?

Customer Morning is best, if that's all right.

Assistant That's fine. So it should be with you on *Monday*, madam.

Customer Good. Thank you very much. Bye.

Assistant Goodbye, madam.

Speaking skills

1
Students' own answers.

2
Students' own answers.

3
Students' own answers.

4

Possible answers

c   To what extent will the Internet mean the end of shopping as we know it?

d   To what extent are people worldwide becoming more materialistic?

e   In what ways is shopping today a less personal process than shopping in the past?

f   What is the purpose of advertising?

g   In what ways does discarded packaging cause environmental problems? / How does discarded packaging cause environmental problems?

h   What are the main differences between shopping in local markets and shopping in big stores? / Which do you prefer, shopping in local markets or shopping in big stores?

5

Speaker 1: h, Which do you prefer, shopping in local markets or shopping in big stores?
Speaker 2: g, To what extent is discarded packaging causing serious environmental problems?
Speaker 3: b, In what ways can shopping be a form of relaxation?

Script
Speaker 1 I suppose that the main difference is that it's set up to be a lot more convenient. It's easy to go and park up at a supermarket and get all your shopping in one go. I know a lot of people don't approve of that. Nevertheless, from my point of view, it's a really good thing. I can save time.
Speaker 2 To my mind, we worry far too much these days about what things are wrapped in. It's all about marketing really. Some customers expect to buy their toothpaste tube in a box, but what's the point? It seems to me that we need to change attitudes about this.

Speaker 3 Well, from my point of view, it's completely the opposite. It just gets me stressed. But I know for a lot of people it's a form of leisure activity. They'd rather wander round a shopping centre than go to a park or the beach. Personally, I think it's a really odd attitude.

6
Speaker 1: I suppose that; from my point of view
Speaker 2: To my mind; it seems to me that
Speaker 3: from my point of view; Personally, I think

7
Students' own answers.

8
Students' own answers.

9
a   Keeping up with the Joneses
b   The fashion cycle
c   You are what you wear

10
Students' own answers.

11
a   In <u>my</u> view,
b   To <u>my</u> mind,
c   It seems to <u>me</u> that
d   <u>My</u> impression is that

12
The pronouns *my* and *me* carry the main stress.

Script
a   In my view, there is too much advertising on television.
b   To my mind, advertising is fun.
c   It seems to me that advertising does more harm than good.
d   My impression is that most advertising is misleading.

13
Students' own answers.

Exam listening
Questions 31–35
31 designers
32 materials
33 fishing
34 waste
35 manufacturing

Questions 36–40
36 information
37 single use
38 value
39 cereal boxes
10 40,000

Script

Lecturer I'm going to begin my lecture today with a look at Product Life Cycles. Now as we go through the Product Life Cycle I will be trying to raise some issues which are important with regard to each phase of the cycle. I won't have all the answers for you this morning. This one of the lecture series is just to get you started and – I hope – interested. Let's start with the first phase of the cycle, that of Product Design. This is really the most important part of the cycle. We often talk as if it is consumers who are responsible for recycling – and so they are – but in reality the major responsibility must be borne by *designers*. They can design products where recycling is easy and cheap, or difficult and expensive. In the latter case, the likelihood is that recycling – though technically feasible – will not, in fact, take place. Now don't jump ahead, because the second stage is not Product Manufacturing, but rather that of *Materials* Acquisition. This is the activity we do when we mine coal or other minerals such as gold or iron or copper. In addition to mining, there is harvesting, which includes the cutting down of trees as a first step in the making of furniture or paper, or *fishing*. These activities have costs which are not only money costs: pollution is one of the extra costs. We have also to think whether the resources we use are renewable – such as trees – or not – such as coal and other minerals. The third stage is not manufacturing either. It is Materials Processing. This is where we take the raw materials and use energy to change them into a form that can be used in manufacturing. For example, trees must be turned into paper, or oil into plastic. The cotton plants that grow in the fields must be turned into cloth. All of these activities require the use of chemical processes and, as with all chemical processes, *waste* is produced – often of a dangerous kind. And now we come to the Manufacturing stage. This is usually the most expensive in terms of cost and energy and waste. The wastes are often those that contribute to global climate change. For example, we make 41 billion glass containers (mostly bottles) each year and we throw most of them away: a lot of *manufacturing* seems unnecessary if we could only organize things better. And this could mean greater profits for the manufacturing companies, too. Stage five is Packaging. Many products are packed in paper or plastic which themselves, of course, have their own processes and costs. Excessive packaging is often criticized, but it must be remembered that packaging serves a purpose – often more than one purpose – such as maintaining freshness and hygiene, as well as providing *information*. In our globalized world, we must never forget the next stage, which is Distribution. This is the stage where transportation and energy play a big part. Lorries, trucks, trains, planes, and ships all use up the precious stocks of oil and, as we know, generate greenhouse gases which, as we hear again and again, contribute to climate change. Stage seven is the point of it all: using the product. Looking after products, using them in the recommended ways, timely repair and maintenance, all reduce the need for early replacement and reduce the number of products in landfill sites. We should not encourage the purchase of *single use* products, that is, products which are designed for use on one occasion only, and then to be thrown away and replaced. I'm going to skip a stage for a moment and move straight on to the final stage which is Disposal – putting the product in the bin. This is the end of the life of the product and we lose it completely. It may have only a little value but it does have a *value* even at this stage of its life, even in fact when it's actually in the landfill site. Now, I missed out one stage. This is a cycle within a cycle. That is, within the life cycle of the product there can be a closed-loop cycle which can extract more value from the product. This is the reuse and recycle loop. It is a closed loop because, in theory, it can continue for ever, though in practice of course, this is not possible. Recycling products means that they can be used to make more of the same product – CDs, bottles, books – or that they can be used to make different ones. For example, one pound of recycled paper can make six *cereal boxes*. And if we recycled all our newspapers, we could save *40,000* trees a day! Now with this approach to the life cycle of a product in mind, we can go on to consider Life Cycle Analysis …

Unit 4

Topic talk

1

a   It is a tutorial. In a tutorial, a lecturer/tutor gives academic advice to a student or a couple of students. In a seminar, a group of students and a lecturer talk about a subject from a lecture or students present a paper on a chosen subject to their peers. In a lecture, students listen to a lecturer talk about a particular subject.

b   Students' own answer.

c   Students' own answer.

2

a   requirements
b   criteria
c   programme
d   module
e   paper
f   portfolio
g   analysis
h   evaluation
i   essay
j   dissertation

3

a   fulfil   f   present
b   meet   g   carry out
c   enrol (on)   h   make
d   choose   i   submit
e   submit   j   submit

4

Possible answers

d   set out your hypothesis and explain your terms of reference

g   state your aims and objectives

f   provide a survey of existing literature

c   describe the methods used for collecting data

a   present an analysis of the data

e   draw conclusions based on your analysis

b   include a bibliography

5

a   background reading list
b   research project
c   easy-going tutors
d   end-of-year examination
e   deadlines; extensions
f   individual tuition
g   ongoing assessment
h   practical work
i   vocational content
j   weekly seminars

6

Students' own answers.

Listening skills

1

a   books, videotapes and DVDs, researchers, librarians, photocopier, indexes

b   study bedroom, kitchen, lounge, bicycles, Internet connection

c   seats, whiteboard, steps, platform, lights, sound system

d   experiment, apparatus, test tube, bench, sink, stool, notes, lab coat

2

Possible answers

1   The most likely place for students to have a discussion is a student flat, followed by lecture theatre and library.

2   The least likely answer is *drinking coffee*, since this is unlikely to take all morning. Perhaps *studying* is the most likely answer.

3

a   at least two, since Bill and Chloe are mentioned by name

b   Bill – question 4 mentions his assignment

c   psychology or education

d   stages in child development

4

1	B	3	C
2	C	4	B

Script

Bill It was packed! There simply aren't enough seats in Theatre 4 – there were people on the stairs, people in the aisles – I don't imagine everybody was able to get in.

Chloe Was Jack with you?

Bill No, of course not. I saw him with a pile of journals in the library as I walked past. You haven't seen him because you've been in here in the kitchen drinking coffee all morning whereas he has been studying hard.

Chloe Not me! I've been in my bedroom reading for my assignment on education in the classical world – very interesting. It was easier than I expected. I should have been at the gym training for my next race, but that'll have to wait. And did you find your first lecture interesting?

Bill Absolutely fascinating! We talked about this experiment: if you show a child a litre of water in a bucket and show him a litre of water in a tall container, he always thinks that the higher, taller, but narrower container has more water in it.

Chloe Hold on, what do you show him?

Bill Right. You show him two things: a bucket … with a litre of water in it. And also, a tall, glass, vase-like thing, or any tall container – this also has a litre of water in it. Now, he will say that the tall thing has more in it than the short fat thing, that is, the bucket. And all children will say this, that is, up to about five years of age. You can then actually pour a litre of water from the bucket into the taller, narrower container and the child will still say that the tall container contains more water – even though he has just seen the water come out of the bucket!

Chloe And what's the point of that? Is it about measurement?

Bill No, it showed how children are quite unable to think logically. It's connected with my assignment. It's about cognitive development of young children over time. That's to say it's about how they think. But didn't you do that assignment last year?
Chloe No, I didn't. You see, I missed out on the first year when I changed subject.

5

Students' own answers.

6

Students' own answers.

7

a Chloe
b her likes and dislikes

8

a	8	d	5
b	6	e	7
c	10	f	9

9

5 second
6 criminal
7 rules and exceptions
8 international trade
9 famous cases
10 practical

Script

Chloe I started psychology in the *second* year – which is where I am now.
Bill Lucky you.
Chloe I'm not so sure. I've missed out on a lot of the basic stuff like that, and I will have to catch up in my own time. So I'm relying on you!
Bill Oh yes, I remember. What did you study before you changed?
Chloe I studied law.

Bill Why didn't you continue?
Chloe I found some of the subjects interesting enough – in fact, the *criminal* area was fascinating in general. But a lot of the law is very technical. It's full of little details, which can be very difficult to understand. And I've got a terrible memory too. I could never get all the *rules and exceptions* into my head. My number one hate really was *international trade* which was a minefield of rules and exceptions – in fact I think it was a complete nightmare!
Bill But law is such a popular subject – lots of people would like to study it.
Chloe I'm sure they would, but they often don't realize that it's very book-based. You spend most of your time reading about *famous cases* sitting in a stuffy library and very occasionally you get out – to a lecture, or maybe a seminar!
Bill What do you find that's better about psychology?
Chloe Most of all I like the experimental psychology we have to study. This involves doing something, so it's *practical*, and with any luck you can make a small – OK very small – contribution to knowledge. And it is so useful in many careers, for example, business, commerce, education …
Bill Law is too, you know.
Chloe Yes, but the training is so long. You have to spend at least another two years on a professional practice course before you can start working. No, I'm happy with psychology.
Bill Well, as a psychology student, too, I must say I agree with absolutely everything you've said, of course …

Speaking skills

1

Students' own answers.

2

Possible answers

They speak many foreign languages.	U
They have a lot of hobbies.	U
They set high standards.	I
They are able to explain difficult things.	I
They tell lots of jokes.	N
They maintain discipline.	I
They avoid negative criticism.	I
They speak loudly.	U
They give a lot of praise.	I
They are very athletic.	N
They mark and return pupils' work quickly.	I
They are good-looking.	N
They know the subject well.	I
They are polite to the pupils.	I

3

Students' own answers.

4

What this teacher looked like: *average height, thin, grey hair, a bun*
What subjects they taught: *all subjects*
What kind of person they were: *quick and precise; a 'yes or no' kind of person*
How this person influenced you: *she taught me how to be firm but kind*

Script

I can remember a teacher called Miss Nicholls really well. She was a teacher I had when I was about six years old. She taught all subjects, not anything in particular. Physically, she was quite ordinary: she was about average height, thin, and with grey hair in a bun. She looked how you would expect for a person of her age – I would say she was about 50 years old. Character-wise, she was quick and precise. She was quick in all her movements, walking and speaking. And she spoke very precisely. She was a 'yes or no' kind of person. Of course, before I moved into her class I was terrified of her. Now, many people have a rough exterior and a soft inside, but the extraordinary thing about Miss Nicholls was that she really did have a heart of gold. I'm sure I'll never forget her because she taught me how to be firm but kind.

5

a The … I've chosen is … ;
  I can remember … really well.
b I'll never forget him/her because …
  What … taught me was that …
c He/she looked … ;
  Physically, he/she was …
d Character-wise, he/she was …;
  In terms of personality, …

6

I can remember … really well.
Physically, she was …
Character-wise, she was …
I'll never forget her because …

7

Students' own answers.

8

physical: short, fat
psychological: amusing, relaxed
habits: looked out of the window while speaking, rolled tie up and down
why good teacher?: made boring subjects interesting, made difficult subjects easy
special quality: cheerful personality

9

a   List A
b   linear note-taking
c   Students' own answer.

10

Students' own answers.

11

a   imagination, imagine
b   motivate, motivation
c   optimistic, pessimists
d   artist, artistic

12

a   imagi<u>na</u>tion, <u>im</u>agine
b   <u>mo</u>tivate, moti<u>va</u>tion
c   opti<u>mis</u>tic, <u>pes</u>simists
d   <u>ar</u>tist, ar<u>tis</u>tic

Script

a   Sarah has lots of imagination and ideas. I can't imagine our office without her.
b   Bill is able to motivate other people and he has a high level of motivation himself.
c   Jack has an optimistic outlook, whereas Tom is one of life's pessimists.
d   Jack is an artist and deals with our publicity. But Tom is very artistic, too.

13

Students' own answers.

Exam listening
Questions 31–35

31 B	34 B
32 B	35 A
33 B	

Questions 36–40
36 agriculture
37 air-conditioning
38 summer school
39 class size
40 parental support

Script

Lecturer So, having seen that the six-term system has passed the test of cost-effectiveness, we can move on to the educational aspects of this arrangement. Firstly, all the terms would be approximately the same length. Instead of terms up to thirteen weeks, which we have now, there could be a repeating pattern of seven weeks of term time plus two weeks of vacation. This would be repeated six times per year. How does this affect the effectiveness of the educational provision? The most noticeable result would be that the very long summer holiday would be reduced in length. This by-product of the six-term system could be beneficial. There is plenty of evidence of huge learning loss by pupils during the summer holidays. By learning loss, we mean the amount that pupils forget – or lose – during a holiday break. Ashley carried out a number of analyses which showed this conclusively. He investigated 39 studies examining the effects of summer holidays on standardized test scores. His analyses indicated that summer learning loss equalled two weeks to seven weeks of instruction. On average, children's test scores were three weeks lower than when they left school in the previous term. He also found differences in the learning loss effect according to subject. The subjects he analysed were reading, writing, and maths, and he found that the effect was greatest in maths and reading. Furthermore, although all social groups experienced roughly similar learning loss in the field of maths, the studies found that disadvantaged children showed even greater losses in reading skills. So the problem of learning loss in traditional schools is clear. However, the results of studies into the six-term system and learning loss are ambiguous. Marchmont found that pupils in six-term schools maintained their test scores after the shorter holiday period. This is certainly an improvement on the traditional system where, as we have seen, pupils perform worse after the summer break. Benson, however, found no differences between those in traditional schools and on the six-term schedule. It would seem reasonable that if long holidays result in learning loss, then shorter holidays should result in less learning loss. So we await the outcome of further studies. Historically, of course, everyone knows the reason for our system of three terms per year. In days when *agriculture* was of much greater importance in our working lives, it was essential that the children helped with the harvest. Later on this changed and more people moved into the towns, but then there was a new problem. Before *air-conditioning*, it was very impractical to try to teach children in the summer months. Nowadays, that's no longer a barrier. One way of providing something different is the *summer school*. Here there is a completely different kind of educational provision. Cooper and others investigated 93 summer schools and the results they achieved. They all had a positive effect on learning. Most summer schools, of course, have small classes and *class size* was shown to have a positive effect. Additionally, summer school children usually benefit from a great deal of *parental support* – not least because payment of fees is involved – and this, as so often, was shown to produce very good outcomes. Results were most impressive in maths in general.

Unit 5

Topic talk

1

Possible answers

a It would probably suit a younger person more, though an older person could also be suitable. Most young people would relate more to someone closer to their age. However, an older person would bring experience.

b Young people have a lot of energy. Young people require a lot of activity to help them develop themselves and occupy their time, so the applicant needs to be enthusiastic. Anyone in charge of young people needs to be dependable and sensible.

c Students' own answer.

2

2	f	6	i
3	h	7	e
4	a	8	d
5	b	9	g

3

a approachable
b well-mannered
c smart
d trustworthy
e educated
f smart
g accomplished
h adult
i lively

4

a unfriendly
b inarticulate
c scruffy
d careless
e uneducated
f slow
g inexperienced
h childish
i apathetic

5

Closed a, b, d
Open   c, e, f, g, h

6

a Part 3
b Part 3
c Part 3
d Part 1
e Part 3
f Part 3
g Part 3
h Part 1 or Part 3

7

c There are many problems, but perhaps the greatest challenge is …
e The most likely development is that …
f By far the best way to tackle the situation is … because …
g The main difference is …

8

Students' own answers.

Listening skills

1

a the post office
b the shopping mall
c the shopping mall

2

1	c	4	e
2	f	5	a
3	d	6	b

3

1	c	3	b
2	a		

4

a It is beside the breakfast tent/ near the breakfast tent.
b It is between Campsite 1 and the disabled viewing.
c It is between the stage and the Olde England Pub.
d It is near the disabled viewing.

5

1	D	3	B
2	E		

Script

Manageress Good morning everybody. I'd like to welcome you to the Castle Pop Festival. My name is Sandy and I'm the general manager of Castle Pop Entertainments and I just want to take a few moments to mention a few things to you before you go and have your detailed briefings in your work groups. You all have a copy of the plan of the festival grounds. Now most things are obvious, but I'd like to point out first the visitor toilets here along the side of the main area. Kindly do not use these yourselves – your own facilities, the staff toilets, are beside the breakfast tent. Also, there are public telephones behind the stage. I mention these two things because they are places that visitors often ask for. For yourselves, one of the most important places is the staff meeting point. This is new this year and the only thing to remember is that it exists and that when you refer to a meeting point between yourselves you need to make clear which one you are talking about. The staff meeting point is between Campsite 1 and the disabled viewing area. This is not marked on the general maps but it is marked on the maps you've got there. The visitors' meeting point is, as you can see, in the centre of the main area, between the breakfast tent and the entrance. Now another important facility is the first aid tent. This is a big round tent so you can't miss it. It's on the right hand side of the entrance – again, as you come in. There are many other first aid facilities all over the festival site. In fact, there is a first aid box in every tent and sales point, but this is the central point. Finally, I wanted to mention the security on the site. Every year the festival gets bigger and bigger and so every year we have to increase the security arrangements. We have a number of small security offices, one being near the entrance, but the main security office is opposite the disabled viewing area – it's next to the Olde England Pub so that the officers can keep an eye on what's going on there. And of course, in that office there is a full supply of first aid equipment, too. And don't forget, those of you who can't wait till you get your pay at the end of the festival, there are some cash machines in the wall of the Olde England Pub.

6

a   the history of the festival
b   4 is an event; 5 is a thing; 6 is a place
c   The clock times are to some extent predictable, because they must be reasonable in the context of organizing a pop festival.

7

4   pop concert
5   castle
6   fields
7   3.15
8   entrance gates
9   8
10 Campsite 1

Script

Manageress I do hope you will enjoy working with us this year. It's always good to see some of last year's faces back with us again. We hope this year to put on an even better festival than before. The first year we put on a festival we called it the Mountain View Pop Concert. And it was a *pop concert* rather than a festival. We held it inside the castle and you could see the mountains in the background. It was very small and personal. Then we held it in front of the castle, with the *castle* in the background and then we started calling it the Castle Festival. Now, this year we have moved further away into the *fields*. The advantage is that the castle and the mountains are both there in the distance, but we have as much space as we want in the fields. The only problem with the fields is that sheep use the fields during the spring months and they leave little messages for us all over the place. So please be careful and encourage the visitors to be careful, too. Now it just remains for me to let you know the times of your detailed briefings which are as follows.

And I'm telling you these as they are not – I repeat not – as written down on your welcome letters. Those of you who are working on the Children's Zone, your meeting is at 2 p.m. in Campsite 2. Those of you on the security team need to meet behind the stage at *3.15* p.m. For the people on first aid, please do not meet in the first aid tent – there will not be enough room – but meet at the *entrance gates* at 4 p.m. Finally, we need everybody, and I do mean everybody, on duty on Monday morning at *8 a.m.* for the final clean-up. I'd like to remind you that Monday is the final day of work, not the Sunday. People not coming to the final day will lose 50 per cent of their pay. The meeting place for that is *Campsite 1*. Now, good luck and let's make this the best festival ever!

Speaking skills

1

Possible answers

a   These are jobs, not careers.
b   A career is long-term, perhaps with promotion and personal development.
c   All of them are suitable for a student.
d   Students' own answer.
e   Students' own answer.

2

Possible answers
Pay
1   pop star
2   dentist
3   shop assistant
4   bus driver
Social usefulness
1   dentist
2   bus driver
3   shop assistant
4   pop star

3

Students' own answers.

4

Possible answers

architect: high job satisfaction, long training, social usefulness
nurse: social usefulness, long training
company director: high pay, variety of job activities, good pension
politician: variety of job activities, risk, high pay
doctor: expensive training, long training, social prestige
social usefulness, good pension, high job satisfaction
schoolteacher: long holidays, high job satisfaction, social usefulness
chef: high job satisfaction
footballer: social prestige, high pay, excitement, risk

5

a Speakers 1 and 3
b Speaker 2
c Speakers 1 and 3

Script

Speaker 1 There are pros and cons with taking a job while studying. On the one hand, you earn money, which is useful. On the other, the job interferes with your study, which is a disadvantage. On balance, I'd prefer not to do a job, but I have to.

Speaker 2 I've been a nurse for twenty years. The disadvantage with nursing is that it is hard work and the pay is not great, but the great advantage is that I can choose my hours and work as many – or as few – as I want. So, overall, I'm happy to continue working.

Speaker 3 The plus is, of course, the wages you can earn, although students often don't earn a lot. Another advantage is the work experience which sometimes can be very useful – meeting the right people and so on. The minus

is the time you have to spend working instead of studying. Weighing everything up, I'd say 'Only work if you have to'.

6

a pros and cons
b on the one hand; on the other
c on balance
d the disadvantage with … is that
e the great advantage is that
f overall
g the plus
h the minus
i weighing everything up

7

Possible answers

Travelling alone
a, b, c, g, h
Travelling with other people
d, e, f, i

8

Students' own answers.

9

Students' own answers.

10

Students' own answers.

11

a hard-working, hard-working
b well-paid, well-paid

Script

Jack is a very hard-working manager.
All Harvey's store managers are hard-working.
Jack is a well-paid accountant.
Most accountants are well-paid.

12

a Before a noun – as in *well-paid accountant* – there is a main stress on the first syllable: well-paid.

b When the word is on its own or after a verb – as in *Most accountants are well-paid* – the main stress is on the second word: well-paid.

13

Students' own answers.

Exam listening

Questions 1–3

1 G   3 D
2 F

Script

Accommodation officer Well, you have left things a bit late. Have you tried looking for somewhere in Newbridge?

Student Newbridge? No, I haven't. I've never heard of Newbridge.

Officer Well, let me show you – I've got a map here. Here's where everything is. You come into Newbridge over the bridge and the main road in front of you is, surprisingly enough, the High Street. This is one of the main streets.

Student Mmm …

Officer And branching off to the left, you can see there, is West Street – that is another busy part of town.

Student I see.

Officer Now, as I was saying, here is the High Street and here is West Street going left. Now if you go along West Street, the first place you come to on your right is the supermarket – it's not a very big one but it's got most things you're likely to need. Next to it, there's the old town hall – I say the old town hall because it is about a hundred years old, but it will soon make way for a car park, I'm afraid. I suppose the car is king. Now opposite the supermarket is the railway station. You can get very frequent buses and trains from here in to the university. And next to that is the sports centre – it's a brand new one and was built on the site of some tennis courts, so that's progress. It's got everything the keen sportsman like yourself might require. Now that's the centre of town and I want to point out to you the buildings opposite the supermarket, but on the other side of London Road. There are two buildings there: the one further away from the High Street is called The Heights and the one nearer the High Street is called The Towers.

Student What are they?

Officer They are where you could find a flat. One of them – The Heights – has a number of flats for rent at the moment.

Student Oh good.

Questions 4–8

4	A		7	C
5	C		8	A
6	B			

Questions 9 and 10

9 clothing factories
10 housing estates

Officer Now the first one is Flat 4. That's a nice flat with a balcony and you need to apply to The Newbridge Accommodation Agency to ask about that one. You'll find their number in the phone book. Number 6 is another nice one which has been empty for a while and you can ring the owner directly, I think … yes, I've got her number written here – there it is.

Student Right, thank you.

Officer Good. Now, number 8 is a re-advertisement –

Student What do you mean?

Officer Well, it did have a tenant, but now it is for rent again, so I'd like to ask about that one. Leave it with me and I'll look into it for you, then we can talk about it when I've got more information.

Student OK … are there others in this block?

Officer Yes, there's number 10, now this one's a bit strange. It's advertised with an agency as well as privately in the local

paper. Normally, if it's advertised through an agency, you shouldn't really go behind the agency and go directly to the owner, but on this occasion I suggest you just answer the advert here in the newspaper which the owner has obviously put in.

Student OK.

Officer Finally, there is number 14. This is with the Newstart Agency – this is an agency started by the girl who was my assistant here and she left to make money for herself, so she's not my favourite person, but I'm afraid I would have to advise you to go through the agency anyway. Again, their number is in the phone book. All right, is that something for you to be starting with?

Student That's great. But what kind of place is Newbridge?

Officer It's a nice place. It was developed about a hundred years ago, really for people who worked in the factories around there. They were clothing factories and everyone worked in them – men, women, boys, and girls. Then when the factories closed down things got very difficult for the town – there was a huge amount of unemployment, until a few years ago when in the telecoms boom a company making mobile phones started up – I think your phone was made in Newbridge – and now this company employs most of the people in the town. There are new housing estates on the edge of the town but they are mostly occupied by young families, and there isn't much student accommodation there. Most flats and so on are in the centre.

Student That sounds good.

Officer Well, let me know how you get on.

Student Yes, of course. Thank you. Bye.

Officer Bye.

Unit 6

Topic talk

1

Possible answers

a The culture of a country is clearly reflected in its buildings and architecture. Otherwise, buildings would be the same throughout the world.

b It is very important, because they are part of each country's heritage. Moreover, they are a source of tourist revenue.

c Students' own answer.

d Traditional buildings can have modern additions, or, if they are of special interest, they can be renovated with modern interiors.

2

a How popular are modern buildings in your country?

b Is the architecture here the same as in your home country?

c Do you prefer traditional or modern architecture?

d Is there any kind of building which you don't like?

e Do you have any buildings of special significance in your country?

f Has the type of building changed since you were a child?

g What kinds of building appeal to you most?

3

1	d		5	g
2	e		6	f
3	c		7	a
4	b			

4

1	c		5	g
2	e		6	f
3	d		7	a
4	b			

5

Students' own answers.

6

a dislike/hate
b would rather
c prefer
d stand
e appeal
f adore
g dislike/hate

7

Possible answers

a I much prefer reading
   contemporary books to classic
   literature.
b Plays in the theatre appeal to
   me more than outdoor drama.
c I am fond of films on DVD, but
   I have to say that I prefer films
   in the cinema.
d I would rather experience
   urban living than country life.
e I adore popular music, but I
   don't mind classical either.
f I can't stand keeping a diary
   except for writing a blog.
g I don't hate art films. I
   just prefer Hollywood
   blockbusters.

Listening skills

1

a Layout B is easier to follow.
b Bold in title; italic type in
   subheadings; indentation for
   detailed information; lettering
   for the first list of points;
   bullet points for items in the
   survey; capitals for subsections
   of *survey type*; underlining to
   emphasize *relative*; headings
   and titles throughout for
   organization.

2

Possible answers
Fiji

Name of country	Fiji
Capital	Suva
Population	800,000
Ethnic composition	a. Fijian
	b. Asian Indian
Climate	hot and wet
Official language	English
Crops	1 sugar
	2 coconuts
Resources	gold

3

a Culture and Society
b six
c Study, Sample, Questionnaire,
   Three examples of statements,
   Examples of results, General
   conclusion
d with a final recommendation
   for further study
e The following are to some
   extent predictable: 1 is the
   name of something; 2 is
   a number, the size of the
   sample; 3 is a number; 4 is
   perhaps an abstract noun; 5
   is a concrete noun, perhaps
   plural; 6 is the name of
   something; 7, 8, and 9 are
   nationalities; 10 is perhaps a
   word like *proved, confirmed,
   supported, contradicted, negated,*
   or *rejected.*

4

1 materialism
2 556
3 7/seven
4 money
5 expensive things
6 possessions
7 Japanese
8 American
9 Chinese
10 not supported

Script

Lecturer Having referred briefly
to the general definition of
culture, I want to move on to an
example of cultural research in
action – a real example of what
researchers into culture are doing.
This is a study done in 2004 into
the 'global teenager hypothesis'.
Now the global teenager
hypothesis states that the values
and attitudes of teenagers all
over the world have become very
similar, that teenagers are part
of a global culture, rather than a
national or a regional one. This
study investigated the subject
of *materialism* in three different
cultures. It asked if teenagers'
attitudes to materialism were
similar or different in those
three different cultures. I'd like
to go through the main points
of this study because I think
it demonstrates the interest
and usefulness of this kind of
research. The research took
a sample of *556* high school
students of between fourteen
and seventeen years of age
from three countries. The three
countries – being also three
differing cultures – were China,
Japan, and the USA. The high
schools were in medium-sized
cities and the students came from
middle-class areas. There were
172 respondents from China,
168 from Japan and 216 from
the USA. The students were
asked to reply to a questionnaire
(or survey) which consisted of
seven statements. They were
asked to say if they agreed or
disagreed with the statements.
The questionnaire was filled
in during the students' regular
class time. I'll give you some
examples of the statements in
the questionnaire. And by the
way, if you want to look into this
in further detail – I've got the
reference here, let me see, oh
yes, it's The International Journal
of Consumer Studies, Volume
28, Number 4, of September
2004. The first statement was:
It is really true that *money* can
make you happy. Respondents
were asked – as they were asked
about all the statements – to give
their answer on a scale of one to
seven. One on the scale indicated
'I strongly disagree'; four on the
scale was neutral; and seven on
the scale was 'I strongly agree'.
The second statement was: My

dream in life is to be able to own *expensive things*. And the fifth was: Having the right *possessions* is the most important thing in life. Let's look at some of the results. With regard to the first statement, it was the *Japanese* teenagers who agreed most strongly that money could make you happy. The Americans were second and the Chinese agreed least. However, regarding one's life dream being to own expensive things, it was *American* teenagers who agreed most strongly with this and the Chinese who agreed least. As regards the fifth statement, – about owning the right things – the Americans agreed less strongly than the other two groups. It was the *Chinese* who agreed most strongly with this statement. I haven't been able to analyse all aspects of the study in this lecture, but it does suggest that the hypothesis is *not supported* by the data. It may be that the culture of the USA is more individualistic, whereas the Chinese culture is more collectivist or communitarian. However, it does not seem to support the global teenager hypothesis. As always, this is something on which we need to carry out more research.

Speaking skills

1

a The first diary is an appointments diary, written in advance. The second is a record of events, written afterwards.
b The film was better because the diary says so. Apart from that, we cannot be sure.
c Students' own answer.
d Students' own answer.

2

1 golf, ice hockey, tennis, football
2 stamp-collecting, gardening, chess, going to concerts

3 meeting friends, going to parties, chatting on the phone, shopping, going to concerts

3

Students' own answers.

4

Speaker 1: listening to music, going to the cinema, going to the theatre (favourite).
Speaker 2: gardening, growing vegetables (favourite)
Speaker 3: sports, rugby (favourite)

Script

1

Interviewer What do you like doing in your free time, Charlotte?
Charlotte I like listening to music and going to the cinema, but my favourite thing of all is going to the theatre.
Interviewer Why do you like that best?
Charlotte What attracts me most is that it is live. It is that these people have come to this place, on this day to perform for us. That's the great thing about theatre.

2

Interviewer What do you like doing in your free time, Deborah?
Deborah I enjoy being outdoors, but best of all I like gardening.
Interviewer Gardening?
Deborah Yes. One thing I like about gardening is that I can do it at home. And the other thing is that I can give a lot, or a little time to it. Also, I can do it for fun or competitively – the thing I like most is growing vegetables and entering them in competitions. But some years, I only have a little time and then I do it for fun, for enjoyment only.

3

Interviewer What do you like doing in your free time, Edward?

Edward I like sports in general. I find them relaxing. Best of all, I like rugby.
Interviewer You find rugby relaxing?
Edward Yes, I really find it relaxing. You see, I work very hard all week at a desk in an office, and in my free time I like doing something completely different.

5

Expressing preferences
I *like* listening to music.
I *enjoy* gardening
My *favourite* thing of all is going to the theatre.
Best of *all*, I like gardening.
Explaining preferences
What *attracts* me *most* is that …
I can do it *for* fun or *for enjoyment*.
I *find* it relaxing.
One thing I *like about* gardening is that …
And *the* other *thing* is that I can …
That's *the great* thing about …

6

Students' own answers.

7

Students' own answers.

8

1 d   3 a
2 c   4 b

9

a The speaker knows little or nothing about the topic of the question.
b a: future hopes; b: past experience; c: natural ability and past experience; d: natural ability and past experience
c a: *I'm afraid*; b: *That's not something I normally do*; c: *Unfortunately not*; d: *I wish I could*.

10

Students' own answers.

11

Students' own answers.

12

a present intention
b something the speaker feels
   he/she should do
c something the speaker enjoys
   doing

13

Script

a I like to have coffee at eleven.
b I'd like to have coffee at
   eleven.
c I'd like to redecorate my
   house to make it look
   beautiful.
d I like to redecorate my house
   to make it look beautiful.
e I'd like to get up early.
f I like to get up early.

14

Students' own answers.

15

David Do you take golf lessons
to improve your game?
Susan Oh yes. I like to take
lessons if I have the time, but I
like playing the game even more!
David Do you have any
ambition in golf?
Susan Yes. I'd like to win the
annual championship at my club!

Exam listening

Questions 21–26

21 C	24 B
22 C	25 A
23 B	26 C

Script

Tutor Come in, sit down. Good
to see you.
Denis, Emily Hello.
Tutor Now, this assignment, the
best thing we can do, I think, is
to think how we can approach it.
The main point is to investigate
television, but not what's
happened in the past.

Emily I was thinking that it
would be necessary to go over the
new media first and then …
Tutor Yes, that's a way to make
a start, but you need to do that
quite briefly …
Emily But it's quite a complex
topic …
Tutor I agree, but the
emphasis must be on the future
development of television as a
cultural phenomenon.
Emily Yes. I've been reading the
talk by Ashley Highfield.
Tutor All right, and what do
you take from that, what are the
things that are competing with
television?
Emily Well, to start with, there
is the games console. Then there
is the personal computer and the
Internet. Then again, the mobile
phone, with its capability of
games and puzzles and, of course,
Internet access. Lastly, there is
the iPod, with the possibility of
listening to music wherever you
go.
Tutor Good, you've understood
that. Now which of these presents
the greatest competition for
television?
Emily Well, according to the
research, it's video games.
Tutor Yes, that's true at present,
but in the future …
Denis I think the phone will
present the greatest threat then
…
Tutor And why? Because
it's mobile, portable, and it's
developing fast. Yeah I think
you're right. You need always
to look to the future and try to
assess how things will develop, as
we said. Good. Now, you need to
move on to the new social trends
in connection with television.
Emily Is one of them the idea
that programmes might become
shorter and shorter?
Denis Ah, yes, the average
programme might be ten minutes
…
Tutor … or even less, just
mini-programmes, say, four to

five minutes long. Now, do you
think you can get access to all the
materials you need?
Denis The problem at the
moment is the library.
Tutor Oh yes. What's happening
there?
Denis There's a tremendous
amount of noise because of the
new extension they are building.
It's quite impossible to work
there.
Tutor They are stopping work
for a week next week, I believe,
and then all the sections will be
open. There's a hold-up because
some roof tiles have not arrived,
so there will be peace for that
week.
Emily But then after that the
Media Studies section will be
closed for a week, and all the
noise and dirt will start up again.
Tutor Yes. But the Sociology
section will be open and there's
some good stuff there for you on
this topic and it's further away
from the noise.
Denis Yes, I don't think the
Sociology section is affected at
all and neither is the Journals
section.
Tutor No, obviously they are
rotating the closures and it was
Sociology's turn to close for a
week last term.
Denis I think we should make a
complaint.
Tutor Yes, I think you should.
Denis I've had a word with
the library staff – they are very
sympathetic but …
Emily They are affected by these
works just as we are.
Tutor If I were you I'd make a
complaint directly to the Premises
Committee. They only meet once
a year but in fact I know they are
having a meeting next Tuesday.
You might like to make contact
with them, but don't say that I
suggested this!
Emily Yes … but the Students'
Union might be better, since they
are independent of the University.

Denis That's true but I can't imagine that people haven't already approached them about this. Let's try the Premises Committee.

Tutor Good idea – why not?

Emily OK.

Tutor Now don't forget I need a copy of your dissertations by email and two copies in print, that is, on paper. If you give the reprographics office 24 hours' notice they'll make copies for you, and if you give them my details they'll send those copies directly to me. They won't send copies to you, so you'll need to take your own copy personally from them. Good. Any questions?

Questions 27–30

27 a podcast
28 Culture and Society
29 the University Theatre
30 4 July

Script

Emily One little thing was just that I wondered whether we should actually talk about that famous website. You know the one: 'youtube'.

Tutor I was rather hoping you hadn't overlooked that. Good point. It's mostly homemade videos. I suppose you could say that each video is a television version of *a podcast*. Anything else?

Denis Yes, I've got a question, I'm afraid. I'm not completely clear about the exact meaning of culture, as we are using it in this subject.

Tutor Well, Mrs Jones is giving a lecture on *Culture and Society* in *the University Theatre*. It's on Wednesday at 10 a.m. and you can learn all about it there, I am sure.

Denis Can you give us that again, please?

Tutor Yes. That's Culture and Society. It's in the University Theatre. And let me just check the time, yes, here it is, 10 a.m. on Wednesday. She'll be giving a very thorough discussion of the issues in defining what culture means.

Denis Right. That's good. The thing is, the reading list confused me a bit. One thing that occurred to me was that it might be broken down into subsections for future students.

Tutor Yes, that's a fair point. I'll bear that in mind. Now don't forget, you need to do the reading, and finish the assignment by *4 July*. Is that OK?

Emily Fine. Thank you very much.

Unit 7

Topic talk

1

a Possible answer
   I think some people are naturally inclined to the arts or sciences, but the environment also plays a part. For example, it is difficult to imagine scientists playing the roles that some actors play, and vice versa.
b Students' own answer.
c Students' own answer.

2

b accomplished
c rigorous
d original
e talented
f expressive
g impartial
h creative
i curious

3

b accomplishment
c rigour
d originality
e talent
f expressiveness
g impartiality
h creativity
i curiosity

4

Possible answer
Someone who is involved in the arts has to have talent, because it is not easy to entertain people if one doesn't have a special gift for doing so. For example, it is not everyone who can stand on a stage and sing a song or make people laugh.

5

a hall of residence regulations
b examination rules and regulations
c assignment guidelines
d assessment criteria
e society/club constitution
f set of instructions
g assignment deadline
h application

6

not optional   requisite
mandatory   imperative
obligatory

7

Possible answers

a It is essential in order to gain good marks and to help prepare for work in later life. Assignments help prepare people for independent work in the real world.
b Visuals help to illustrate ideas. Because a picture says more than a thousand words, they are desirable but not essential, especially if one is a good speaker.
d A bibliography shows which materials, such as books and journals, have been looked at as sources. This is important because other people can then follow up the ideas elsewhere if they want to.
e Preparation is vital because it reduces the amount of work later on. What's more, in order to illustrate one's approach it is essential to have many

ideas, facts and figures to hand. For example, it would be difficult to write about a historical event without knowing the background facts.

f   At least one draft is strongly advisable, if not essential. In order to refine one's ideas, it is sometimes necessary to rewrite something three or four times.

g   The key to preparing a good assignment is addressing the whole question, since it is easy to overlook an important part of the task.

h   In order for a lecturer and fellow students to follow what is being said, it is important to speak clearly and naturally. Organization is also a prerequisite, if fellow students are to extract information. Because technology is in every part of the curriculum, it is essential for students to be completely computer literate.

Listening skills

1
a   science; visits to a festival
b   student teachers

2

Possible answers
2   How long should the student teachers arrange the visits to last?
3   What is the most important purpose of the festival visits?
4   What are the central features of our scientific age?

3
1 C   4 A
2 A   5 B
3 B

Script
Lecturer Now I think nearly all of you have received confirmation of your school placements for next term, and as part of your activities we will be asking you to take responsibility for promoting a school visit to the Norchester Science Festival. Of course, the head of science at your school will be aware of the festival and should have all the details of it, but all the heads of science at your schools will be looking to you to be the main organizer and motivator of a visit to the festival. They'll give you the documents you need. We hope that you will motivate pupils at your schools to take an interest in the festival. It runs for three days. There are day tickets and special three-day tickets, and schools have the extra option of a two-day ticket. We hope you will encourage your pupils to visit it on one or two days. But most important of all, we hope you will use the festival to generate a lively interest in science that will last all year round and provide the school with a lasting benefit. This will, with luck, lead to improved examination results in science subjects. And let's not forget – we hope your pupils will have a lot of fun, too. Needless to say, your performance in achieving these aims will count towards your final exam grade at the end of the year. Now, let me just say a few words on why a science festival. Science is part of our everyday world in a way that is different now from before. Of course we are used to having the benefit of scientific inventions; we are used to the aeroplane, the motorcar, the space rocket and so on. But now we live in a truly scientific age, which means one where inventions and improvements are matters of routine rather than occasional and unusual events. We have become a really scientific society. Yet we find that we are failing to interest and enthuse the young in this. Fewer young people are choosing to study science at school after the age of sixteen, and even fewer at university. As a result we have fewer teachers coming into schools to teach science. And many science teachers are not teaching their specialism. For example, I know of several cases where maths is being taught by biologists and chemistry is being taught by physicists. We urgently need another 3,000 science teachers in England, at least. That's why we look to you, the science teachers who are starting off your careers, to inject enthusiasm and wonder into the study of science. And we hope the Norchester Festival will help you to do this.

4
Chapter 1: c
Chapter 2: a
Chapter 3: e
Chapter 4: b
Chapter 5: d

5
a   journey through the past centuries
b   celebrated
c   studying the stars
d   innovations
e   catastrophes

6
a   types of events
b   that these are titles of events
c   the list A–E – it would not normally be possible to paraphrase the proper names and titles in the other list.
d   Possible answers
     a show:
     a performance, an entertainment, an act
     an event of local interest:
     regional, a district, an area, interest, importance
     a technical demonstration:
     an explanation, an example, a working model

an open discussion:
a conversation, a round table, a debate, contributions
a participation activity:
all invited, to join in, everyone, take part

7

6	B	9	E
7	D	10	C
8	A		

Script

Lecturer Now, enough of the background, what about the festival? There are three main venues where the festival events take place. These are the Millennium Library, the town hall – not the town hall itself but the town hall Conference Centre – and the Norchester Theatre. Now when you are planning your visits, remember that many of the activities for younger pupils will be at the Millennium Library, and the secondary school pupils may find more to interest them in the Conference Centre. Now just so that you have some immediate information, I'd like to mention a few of the events that are taking place this year. One event of special interest to people living in this area is called *Waterworld*. This is a clay model of the south-east of England and the presenters show you the effects of rising sea levels as a result of climate change. They ask the audience to select the rise in sea level, for example 20 or 40 or 60 centimetres, and the model shows the places that would be flooded as a result. Watch out for your town – does it sink or does it swim? *Transport 2050* is about transport options for our towns in the future. A number of experts will introduce the topic, and then everyone at the event will have a chance to speak and give their views. *Science in a suitcase* is a comedy act by two scientists who do crazy experiments and sing songs and play the clown to large audiences every afternoon. I'm particularly looking forward

to that one, which should be entertaining. *Ropes and hangings* is an interactive event which will be of interest to young people in which, after experimenting with ropes and bricks, they build a real suspension bridge. That kind of hands-on activity is always really popular. And, appealing to a different audience, there is *Paper and time* in which some experts will be showing us the techniques they use for the conservation of ancient books and manuscripts. This will obviously not be for everybody, but it should be interesting just to see how they do it. Now, let's move on to tickets and transport to the festival.

Speaking skills

1

a   In the first case, the accident was the head becoming separated from the stand. In the second case, the accident was forgetting about the liquid.
b   Students' own answer.

2

Possible answer

Sciences
numeracy
analytical
demonstration
discipline
knowledge of the universe
experiment
certainty
incremental
definite
Arts
knowledge of humanity
performance
creative
mysterious
literacy
work of art
imagination
original
uncertainty

3

Students' own answers.

4

a   comparison
b   evaluation
c   evaluation
d   comparison

5

a   2 and 4
b   1, 3, and 6
c   1, 3, and 6
d   4 and 6

6

Students' own answers.

7

Students' own answers.

8

Speaker 1: c
Speaker 2: a
Speaker 3: b

Script

Speaker 1 Well, some people would say that it's a great help in that lots of tasks are much easier than they were in the past. I'm not sure because some gadgets create a lot of work in themselves to maintain. And we end up just finding other new chores to take up the time.

Speaker 2 It's often said that the arts offer something to society, and therefore it's in everyone's interests if they get funding from the state. That's not my view, because, if they were really that important, people would just be happy to pay higher ticket prices. Besides, if there was no funding, it would force them to think more commercially.

Speaker 3 There is an argument that scientists are too isolated: that they work in specialized departments and don't really think about the consequences of their ideas on the world outside. I really don't think that's true. I mean, things have changed, and a lot of scientists are interested in how their work is seen by non-specialists

9

Speaker 1: a
Speaker 2: e
Speaker 3: f

10

Speaker 1: Well some people would say that …
Speaker 2: It is often said that …
Speaker 3: There is an argument that …

11

Speaker 1: I'm not sure because …
Speaker 2: That's not my view, because …
Speaker 3: I don't really think that's true.

12

Students' own answers.

13

We pronounce *the* with /schwa symbol/ when it is followed by a consonant sound, eg *the machine*, *the technology*. We pronounce *the* with /i:/ when it is followed by a vowel sound, eg *the accident*, *the experiment*.

Script

the arts and the sciences

14

The words to be circled are in bold.

Script

a People say **that** science will provide the answers to all our problems, but I don't think that outcome is very likely.

b **There** are many inventions which came from China in the distant past, and now a lot of brilliant scientists are working there.

c Some scientific inventions have resulted in great harm; others have resulted in **some** useful labour-saving products.

Exam listening

Questions 21–25

21 330
22 access
23 everyone
24 value for money
25 recovery

Script

Briony What have you been working on, Arthur?
Arthur I've been looking into the funding of the arts by the Arts Association.
Briony Oh, Mr Simpson gave you that topic, did he?
Arthur Yes, it's not too difficult. At least all the facts and figures are easy to find, or I think they will be. I've done a lot of useful stuff already. Simpson hasn't asked me to present my research for the past few seminars, so I think he might ask me this time.
Briony Well, what have you found out?
Arthur Well, it's big money at the Arts Association. £*330* million from the government and £118 million from the Lottery. Let me see, I've got my notes here. Now, the Arts Association mission statement tells us that it exists to develop, sustain, and promote the arts. So that's clear, but then we need to know exactly how it can do this. However, before we get to that, there are certain issues which the Association must take into account.
Briony What are those issues?
Arthur They are, first, *access*. This is the idea that the arts mustn't be just for the few.
Briony Not just Italian opera, but pop concerts, too?
Arthur Something like that. Other issues are education, cultural diversity, social regeneration, and social inclusion. All these are different ways of saying that the arts are for *everyone*.
Briony All right, but what does it actually do?

Arthur It does what it wants, I think. The government does not interfere in its activities, but demands that it gets *value for money* for its funds.
Briony But there must be certain programmes that it carries out?
Arthur Oh yes. There is the touring programme, which is what it says, that is, a programme to support …
Briony … give money to …
Arthur … yes, that's right… to support touring companies, for example, dance companies, orchestras and so on. There is also the *recovery* programme.
Briony What on earth is that?
Arthur It's a financial programme to give extra money to organizations which are financially in a bad way or which might have financial difficulties in the future. Like it says, it's for their recovery.
Briony It all seems very complicated.
Arthur It is.

Questions 26–30

26 D	29 C
27 A	30 B
28 F	

Script

Briony Did you get any information on the reading for the other half of our work?
Arthur Yes, I did. You mean the Art and Society module?
Briony Yes.
Arthur Yes. I met Simpson himself as we were waiting for a train at Norchester station so I managed to ask him.
Briony Any luck?
Arthur Yes. I've got the notes I took here. He told me, of course, to start with Greenberg, who covers contemporary art and the up-to-the-minute movements in America. It's about the modern movements really. As far as the economic impact of art is concerned, a basic text is the

Parliamentary report on art and the UK economy. This gives lots of monetary facts and figures, but the figures are not very satisfactory as, of course, a lot of the information is confidential and can't be published. *Art Now! Art Wow!* by someone called Dennison sounds exciting and is about how art and artists are created, presented for buyers, and sold in the US. It's about the whole trade in art as a phenomenon.

Briony Like a product, like washing powder …

Arthur Yes … . That's the idea of the book, anyway. And there's another one here, oh yes, by someone called Hampton. It's a book called *American Art* which Simpson says is full of discussion on the relationship of art to the other aspects of culture, such as film, television, books and so on.

Briony Popular culture, I suppose.

Arthur Not just popular … culture of all sorts, I imagine. Finally, for the spiritual and more abstract aspects of art, he recommends *Art and the Mind of Modern Man* by Frick. It's sort of about how art relates to how we think. He did have lots of other recommendations, but luckily his train arrived before he could move on to them. These seem enough to me.

Briony Yes. They're a good place to start. We will be busy.

Unit 8

Topic talk

1

a   Students' own answer.

Possible answers

b   Places like those in the picture appeal to people because they are idyllic and peaceful. They offer people tranquillity and the space to be themselves.

c   The world is more and more stressful so we need places where we can escape from the problems of general living. People with stressful lives often like to retreat to places like this to relax and unwind. It is also good to think of such places when one is stressed.

2

a   enthusiastic
b   enthusiastic
c   enthusiastic
d   unenthusiastic
e   unenthusiastic
f   unenthusiastic
g   enthusiastic
h   enthusiastic

3

Possible answers

b	2	f	3
c	1, 2, 4, 5	g	1, 2, 4, 5
d	5	h	2, 5
e	5		

4

a   What makes me feel so relaxed there is the silence.

b   What does me a lot of good is being away from the city.

c   What makes the place restful is the fact that there are no shops.

d   What makes the sea clean is the fact that there are no factories.

e   What makes the garden very private is the trees.

f   What makes the area so welcoming is the people.

g   What makes the area appealing is the many tourist attractions.

5

b   Why does it do you a lot of good?

c   Why is the place so restful?

d   Why is the sea so clean?

e   Why is the garden so private?

f   Why is the area so welcoming?

g   Why is the area so appealing?

6

Students' own answers.

7

Possible answers

b   What I recollect most is its playfulness, especially when it was young.

c   What I will always remember is the way it was wrapped.

d   What made me feel so uncomfortable is the fact that there were so many people around.

e   What made it so memorable is the friends that I made on the trip.

f   What made the trip unforgettable is the number of places we managed to visit.

8

Students' own answers.

Listening skills

1

a   Speakers B, C, E, and G.

b   Speaker B: no, I mean …
Speaker C: … in fact.
Speaker E: Actually, you're right.
Speaker G: Yes, that's what I meant.

2

a	5	c	the end
b	2		

3

Questions 1–3: three selections
Questions 4 and 5: two selections

4

Questions 1–3

1	C	3	E
2	F		

Questions 4 and 5

4	C	5	D

Script

Adrian Hello Brenda, how are you doing?

Brenda Fine. I've just come over to talk about this assignment on the function of zoos. Oh, hello, Charles.

Charles Hello, Brenda. That's good. I've just been in the library looking at some stuff. I think Adrian's been on the web.

Adrian Yes, I have.

Brenda Well, that's great. What have you found out about zoos?

Charles I've been looking into the history, both of zoos and of keeping animals generally.

Adrian I didn't think we had to do that.

Brenda Yes, it was one of the topics we had to research. We definitely need to cover it, even if only briefly, I think. After all, people have kept animals for recreation and pleasure for centuries. The ancient Egyptians kept collections of animals, and of course the Romans kept animals for recreation.

Adrian Ah, the Romans. That brings us to the general question of the treatment of animals, and the mistreatment of them …

Charles Yes, but that's not our topic. We've been told to keep off that. Now, where were we?

Brenda Our assignment is concerned with the purposes of zoos in general, and in our modern era. We have to cover the history, but not in great depth. Our main focus is the scientific aspects of zoos, and the work they do for conservation and so on.

Adrian We mustn't forget the question of who pays for them. Zoos are hugely expensive places to run nowadays. There are the costs of feeding the animals obviously, and security, for the animals and the public, what happens if they escaped and so on. We have to ask what benefits we get from this.

Brenda Adrian, I don't think you'll find we have to do that kind of thing at all.

Adrian But I've been looking into all that, and the social benefits of zoos …

Brenda What I mean is, that's not part of this assignment. All this financial and safety stuff is not necessary. We should stick to their purposes. Now, what have you found out, Charles?

Charles Well, I discovered that the World Association of Zoos and Aquariums was very helpful on this. I've got their website address here somewhere. I found out about the scientific research that zoos do. The other thing we should cover is the educational side of their work …

Adrian The educational side is pretty obvious. I've got lots of stuff here about this and more references to websites and information. There's also the area of entertainment. What about that?

Charles He's got a point. I think we need to do some more research on that.

Brenda Fine. But it sounds like we've covered the history and science angles pretty well.

Charles I agree, let's leave those for now and plan some more study on the entertainment stuff.

Brenda And let's do some more work on the conservation element.

5

6 a colour
7 an adjective
8 a date
9 a number
10 an activity

6

6 white
7 hot (desert)
8 1972
9 300
10 illegal hunting

Script

Adrian Oh yes. The Arabian oryx is a classic case.

Brenda The what?

Adrian The Arabian oryx. It's like a deer, but *white*. That is, it has a white body but brown legs, and long curved horns. It normally lives in the *hot* desert in the Arabian peninsular. Anyway, in the 70's the population declined and in *1972* the last wild oryx was shot and it became extinct in the wild. There were a few left in zoos in the United States, where there was a captive breeding programme. This was so successful that in 1982 a small population was reintroduced into the wild. Hunting of wild animals was made illegal and there are now about *300* in Oman.

Charles Although there was a big problem there, I believe. The population went up to about 450 in the 90's and then *illegal hunting* did take place. The population crashed again and the programmes had to be restarted. But that's been successful and there are now, I believe, as you say, several hundred in the wild. This is all available on the websites that Adrian has noted.

Adrian There was a similar programme in Saudi Arabia and I think there are hundreds in the desert there now.

Brenda We can use that as a definite success story.

Adrian And what have you found out?

Charles Yes, what have you come up with?

Brenda I'm going to the library now.

Charles Good.

Speaking skills

1

a dog
b cat
c horse

2

a dog: jump up, wag their tails, bark

b cat: arch their backs, scratch, curl up, purr

c horse: get excited, jump

3

a take them for walks, throw sticks for them

b let them curl up on one's lap, stroke them

c look after them, feed them, groom them

4

a The fondest memory I have is …

b But what I remember most is …

c The thing that sticks in my mind is …

5

a Speaker 2

b Speaker 1

c Speaker 3

Script

Speaker 1 Yes I did, although in fact I wouldn't call him a pet, exactly. Rover was our guard dog, but he had a peculiar way of guarding the house. We had burglars twice and on each occasion he didn't bark or attack the burglars. He ran out of the house to the neighbours' house and barked at their front door. Both times they called the police and the burglars were caught. So in his way he was an excellent guard dog.

Speaker 2 Like most parrots, he was very colourful. I'm not really sure if a parrot is a real pet – they're not very friendly or affectionate. Anyway, he spoke very little, but when he did …!

Speaker 3 My favourite pet animal was Lassie. Really of course, he wasn't my pet at all, but I loved him. I had lots of books about him and, of course, I watched the television programmes whenever I could. I thought he was wonderful.

6

Speaker 1: Although in fact I wouldn't call him a pet, exactly.

Speaker 2: I'm not really sure if a parrot is a real pet.

Speaker 3: Really of course, he wasn't my pet at all.

7

Students' own answers.

8

a Possible answer
   Reminding people who are thinking of giving an animal as a present, that having an animal is a responsibility that lasts as long as the pet lives.

b Students' own answer.

c Students' own answer.

9

Students' own answers.

10

a *Present madness*

b Students' own answer.

c Students' own answer.

11

Candidate 2's notes are more practical because there is only enough time to write about ten words in the one minute available.

12

Students' own answers.

Exam listening

Questions 31–38

31 black or grey

32 trees and buildings

33 insects and fruit

34 170 million

35 nesting

36 commercial crops

37 financial

38 diseases

Questions 39 and 40

39 B

40 C

Script

Lecturer Thousands of exotic plants and animals have been introduced into the British Isles over thousands of years. These newcomers compete with native species for resources, and can also cause major changes in the wildlife and in the habitats of our countryside. The problem is not just British of course, but global, and it has been going on for centuries. One good example of this I'd like to mention today is the European starling. The starling, to us in the UK, is a fairly ordinary little bird, about twelve inches long. In flight it appears to be *black or grey* with tiny white spots. So it's a very ordinary-looking, almost dirty-looking bird. It nests in *trees and buildings* and can be found in the country and in towns. It travels in large flocks, leaving the nests in the morning and returning in the early evening. It feeds on *insects and fruit*. Its native range includes the British Isles and Finland, but it is also found in most of Europe and parts of Asia and Africa. In the British Isles and Finland, however, it has suffered a huge decline, and in these countries there is an effort to conserve the species. It is a different story in some of the places where it has been introduced. For example, the population in the USA is estimated at *170 million* birds. Also, they are becoming a big problem in Australia and New Zealand. Starlings, as I have said, nest in trees and it has been found that they are more aggressive than native species, native that is to Australia and New Zealand, when they are looking for *nesting* places. They therefore compete with native species for nests and also they drive those species away from nests. So, this nest-building activity causes harm to native species, but also they are a nuisance to humans. They gather in large flocks of thousands of birds and feed together on *commercial crops.* This causes great *financial* damage to farmers. And they also make a mess, both in the town and the countryside. There is also the problem that starlings may carry *diseases* which affect both humans and other animals, although this has not been really confirmed and we are waiting for more work to be done on this. The question arises – what are we to do about foreign species which not only do damage to native species but interfere with human activity? We have three approaches in theory, but usually it is not a free choice between them. Usually we have to do the best we can and that money will allow. The best approach of course is prevention, and many countries have passed legislation which attempts to limit or prevent the arrival of non-native species in their countries. In particular, there are many international regulations on how and where ships may pick up and deposit water, and this is a major contribution to preventing the accidental transport of fish and organisms by ship, since accidental transport by ship is a frequent cause of fish and other creatures going from place to place. Ports also have special areas where water can be deposited, and many of them have treatment facilities to kill any foreign species that may establish themselves in their waters. For fish and organisms that live in water, these international regulations are useful, but obviously not all species can be dealt with in this way. Sometimes it is simply too late for prevention. Then we have to consider eradication or management. By management I mean that we have to decide how best to live with the new creatures and how to keep their numbers down. However, this becomes not only a scientific

question. It can be a matter of choice what population level of an invasive species we want to maintain. This choice involves costs: there is the cost of living with the species and there is the cost of managing the species over time (and species management is usually a long-term business without any foreseeable end). However, there is not just the economic aspect to this question. We can also consider the ethical point: how should we treat animals which we have, sometimes deliberately, introduced into the environment? Is it permissible just to exterminate a number of them convenient to ourselves? The most important decision has to be made in the political forum, whatever considerations go into the making of that decision. These questions are relevant also to the approach of eradication which is another option but which does not have an encouraging history. Many attempts have been made to eradicate introduced species …

Unit 9

Topic talk

1
a   Students' own answer.
b   Possible answer
    Football and tennis are more useful, because they use more energy and muscles than golf.
c   Students' own answer.
d   golf: outdoor sports
    football: outdoor sports, team sports
    tennis: racket sports

Other sports
water sports: swimming; water-skiing; sailing; scuba-diving
adventure sports: mountaineering; sky-diving
motor sports: motorcycle racing; karting
blood sports: hunting; shooting

team sports: football; hockey; netball
non-contact sports: swimming; athletics
racket sports: badminton; tennis; squash
indoor sports: basketball; table tennis
outdoor sports: rugby; cricket

2
1	d	4	e
2	f	5	b
3	a	6	c

3
Students' own answers.

4
opponent
opportunity

5
a   makes people mentally alert
b   people get few illnesses
c   people learn new skills
d   you can meet new people
e   people feel more relaxed
f   you can be part of a team
g   there's a competitive atmosphere
h   there are opportunities to be outdoors
Students' own choice of three.

6
1   a, b, e   3   d, f
2   c, g, h

7
Students' own answers.

Listening skills

1

Possible answers
1   language difficulties
2   student debt
3   feeling homesick
4   examination pressure
5   poor accommodation
6   colds and flu

2

Possible answers

a not liking the food
   difficulty in making friends
   not knowing where things are
   finding the work difficult

b feeling homesick
   – Counselling service
   examination pressure
   – Counselling service
   colds and flu
   – Health centre
   poor accommodation
   – Counselling service
   language difficulties
   – Counselling service
   student debt
   – Counselling service

c Students' own answers.

3

a You will read the information
   from left to right, dealing with
   each student service in turn.

b 2, 4, and 5

c 1 is probably a geographical
   expression; 3 is possibly a
   compass direction, such as
   north, south, east, or west.

4

1 yellow
2 8/eight
3 Central
4 0900 7625913
5 £22

Script

Student Hi. I wonder if you
could help me. I'm starting a
course at Glenfield in a few
weeks. I was just a bit worried
about what facilities there will
be and what I'll have to do. I'm
especially interested in health and
welfare stuff.

Advisor Certainly. We normally
send out a copy of our leaflet
'Staying healthy at Glenfield'. I'm
not sure why you haven't had it.

Student Well, could you answer
a few questions for me? Firstly,
I'm wondering about how I get a
doctor when I arrive.

Advisor Well, you can register
with the University Health Centre
on North Campus.

Student And do I have to pay
for that?

Advisor Not to register, but if
you have to get medicines, there's
a prescription charge of £6.50.

Student OK. Well, I'm not
planning to get ill. That's only
going to arise if I have any
problems. So should I just go
along when I arrive?

Advisor That's what we
recommend for peace of mind.
But it's not compulsory, and
if you don't live inside the
catchment area you can't in fact
register there. Where do you live?

Student Well, at the moment
I'm staying at the backpackers'
hostel in Hill Street, but I will
be moving from there shortly.
Somewhere nearer.

Advisor Well, there's a map at
the centre which shows you the
area that the university practice
can accept people from – it's what
we call the *yellow* zone. If you live
outside that area you have to find
another medical centre to register
with.

Student It sounds like I'll only
qualify after I move.

Advisor I think you might
be right. Then, in addition to
the Health Centre, there's a
free Counselling service for all
students situated on the North
Campus. You don't have to
register. They also have drop-in
sessions. I say it's free, but that's
only for up to *eight* sessions.
Beyond that they normally refer
people elsewhere.

Student Sounds serious.

Advisor Well, it's not just for
big problems. People go there for
advice on housing, workload,
whatever really. They can even
arrange financial help.

Student Is it confidential?

Advisor Absolutely. Then again,
a lot of students prefer to phone
the Nightline service, which is
run from an office on the *Central*
Campus. They don't really
encourage people to drop in.

Student I see.

Advisor So it's basically a free
phone line. The number, if you

want to make a note, is *O – nine-
hundred – seven six two – five nine
– one three*. I'll say it again. O
– nine-hundred – seven six two
– five nine – one three.

Student Fine. Well I hope I
won't need any of these. What I
will want is access to some gym
facilities.

Advisor Right. Well, you'll find
those on the South Campus in the
Sports Centre. It's great, but it's
not free. You have to present your
student card and pay a fee of *£22*
to get a pass, but that will last you
for the whole year.

6

List 1	a, h, j, k,
List 2	b, c, d, e, g, p, t, v,
List 3	f, l, m, n, s, x
List 4	i, y
List 5	q, u
List 6	r, o, w, z

7

Date:	(Tuesday) 4th
Time:	2.30 p.m.
Message for:	Susan
Message from:	Jane Smith
Caller's number:	01324 781205

Message: leave birthday present
at 18, Grosvenor Crescent,
Southwark JG8 2AE

Script

I'm afraid I can't take your call at
the moment. Please leave your
message after the tone.

Caller: Hello, erm, as nobody's
there I'll leave a message. Erm,
this is a message for Susan.
Could you please send the
birthday present to this address:
18 Grosvenor Crescent, that's
Grosvenor – G-R-O-S-V-E-N-O-R
– Crescent, Southwark, that's S-
O-U-T-H-W-A-R-K. The postcode
is JG8 2AE. I hope that's clear.
Any problems, please ring me on
01324 781205. Oh, I should say
this is Jane Smith, at around 2.30
p.m. on Tuesday the fourth. Bye.

8

Students' own answers.

9

6 (whole) information pack
7 Sonia Orr
8 Winter Gardens
9 GF23
10 Economics and Sociology

Script

Student Is this information on the website?

Advisor I'm afraid not. I can send you some leaflets or even resend the whole information pack, if you give me your details.

Student Could you send the *whole information pack* please?

Advisor Yes, that's fine. I'll have to take down some details. Could you tell me your full name?

Student *Sonia Orr.*

Advisor S–O–N–Y–...

Student Er, no, I'll spell it. S–O–N–I–A ... then Orr is O–R–R.

Advisor Orr ... OK. And you said you were on Hills Road.

Student Yes, but don't send it there as I'm about to move. I'll give you my new address, which is 22 ... *Winter Gardens*. That's Glenfield.

Advisor And the postcode?

Student Oh yeah. That's *GF23* ...9BQ.

Advisor Fine. Now we're doing a bit of data collection about who uses our services at the moment. Can I just ask a few more questions?

Student Yes, that's fine.

Advisor OK, if you're an international student, what country are you from?

Student I'm from Switzerland.

Advisor And how old are you?

Student I'm 24.

Advisor And finally, which course are you enrolled on?

Student Right, well that's a bit complicated, since I'm hoping to switch to Economics and History.

Advisor But at the moment ...

Student ... I'm down to do *Economics and Sociology.* It's a joint degree.

Advisor OK. I'll put that. Great, well ... I'll pop the information pack in the post and you should get it soon.

Speaking skills

1

a Students' own answers.
b Students' own answers.
c

Possible answers

drinking excessive alcohol; infections; not getting enough fresh air; not maintaining good posture

2

a is similar to g
b is similar to e
c is similar to j
d is similar to f
h is similar to i

3

a, g 2, 4, 5, 8,
b, e 3, 4, 5,
c, j 2, 7, 9, 10
d, f 7, 9, 10
h, i 7

4

Speaker 1: Questions c or j
Speaker 2: Questions b or e
Speaker 3: Questions h or i

Script

Speaker 1 I think it depends on what interests you and how committed you are. I suppose the best way, or at least the most effective way of getting healthy is through doing more exercise. I mean, diet's important, but you can be thin and unhealthy. So yeah, I'd say exercise is the key thing.

Speaker 2 It's difficult to say, I think. There are so many reasons. The main cause seems to be smoking. I mean, it's the biggest cause of early deaths in most countries, I think. What else? Oh yeah, there's also salt. People eat more than they should do. But actually, people are getting more aware now of the dangers.

Speaker 3 I don't really know for sure, but my impression is that it can help. It's obvious that it helps if you think about it because people keep going back for acupuncture and homeopathy. So, it's mostly because of what people believe. That's what makes it effective.

5

It's mostly because of ..., Speaker 3
I suppose the best way is ..., Speaker 2
The main cause seems to be ..., Speaker 2
I'd say ... is the key thing. Speaker 1
I think the most effective way is ..., Speaker 1
It's obvious that ..., Speaker 3

6

b

7

Speaker 1: I think it depends ...
Speaker 2: It's difficult to say, I think.
Speaker 3: I don't really know for sure, but my impression is that ...

8

Students' own answers.

9

a The first article suggests that exercise might have disadvantages. The second article points out that there may be problems with experts' advice on diet.
b Students' own answer.

10

Students' own answers.

12

Script

a Put on *sun*-cream before you
   go out.
   Put on sun-cream be*fore* you
   go out.
b *Thir*ty minutes daily is a good
   amount of exercise.
   Thirty minutes *dai*ly is a good
   amount of exercise.
c Fresh fruit is good for
   *every*one.
   Fresh fruit is good for
   everyone.
d Fish *is* good for the brains of
   children.
   Fish is good for the brains of
   *child*ren.

13

a Men spend thirty minutes a
   day on sport.
b *Wo*men spend fifteen minutes
   a day on sport.
c The life expectancy of *men* is
   seventy-seven years.
d The life expectancy of women
   is eighty-*one* years.

Exam listening

Questions 11–15

11 Meeting Point
12 Changing Rooms
13 Sports Hall
14 First Aid
15 Cafe Lounge

Script

Instructor Good morning
everybody. I'd like to welcome
you to Rose's Health Club which
is part of the nationwide Rose
Group of Health and Fitness
centres. Today I hope to tell you
everything about the Glenfield
centre and the facilities it offers.
First, have a look at the map of
the centre I have put up here
– there's a copy of it in your
information packs. As you can
see we have a range of facilities.
We are here at the *meeting point*,
next to the reception desk. If you
get lost, which is unlikely, make
your way here. The main feature
of the health club is, of course,
the swimming pool. This is a 25-
metre pool divided into three or
four lanes. Access to the pool is
normally through the *changing
rooms*, for obvious reasons. To get
to these, bear left as you come
through reception and, as you
follow the corridor, they are the
two doors immediately to your
right, first the female changing
room, then the men's. If you
follow the corridor right to the
back of the building you'll find
one of our most popular features
– three state-of-the-art squash
courts. We keep them in very
good condition, so if you're keen
on that sport, I'm sure you'll
appreciate the quality. Right
then, I'm sure what many of
you are thinking of joining for
is access to the gym facilities
and activities like yoga. We've
got lots of space for this, and
these are all situated on the left-
hand side of the main corridor,
opposite the changing rooms
and squash courts. At the far
end, you'll find the fixed and
free weights room – there are
lots of fixed weights machines,
and you'll also find exercise
bikes and rowing machines. Next
to that, directly opposite the
changing rooms, there's access
to our *sports hall*. This is where
yoga classes, martial arts, circuit
training, and other classes take
place. We even have badminton
and table tennis sometimes. OK,
moving on from the sports, there
are two other things to point
out. One is a small door next to
reception, to the left as you come
in. This takes you into the staff
training room. This is important
because you'll know where to
find us in an emergency, and
it doubles as a *first aid* room in
those circumstances. Finally, last
but not least, there is another
corridor to the right as you come
in, and that leads you to the
cafe lounge on one side and the
viewing area for the swimming
pool on the other.

Questions 16–20

16 £850
17 250
18 (a) personal trainer
19 during the week/weekdays
20 50%

Script

Instructor Now we will go for
a little tour in a moment, but
first I'd like to tell you a little
about the different kinds of club
membership we have, so that
you can be thinking about what
you want as we go round. We
first of all have the Anytime
membership. Anytime is the
complete go-as-you-please
membership. This entitles you
to full use of all the facilities
during all opening hours. And
we're open every day from 5
a.m. till midnight. This costs
£850 per year, though there are
some discounts which I will tell
you about in a moment. Don't
forget that the Rose Group is
a nationwide group and this
membership also entitles you to
the full use of the group's other
250 clubs around the country.
The Freetime membership is
an off-peak membership. This
entitles you to use of the facilities
between 10 a.m. in the morning
and 3 p.m. in the afternoon.
Also you can use the facilities at
any time at weekends. This costs
£500. Note that you will still
have access to a *personal trainer*
under this membership scheme.
Finally, a Standard membership
costs £400 and is a weekday
membership really, especially
suitable for retired people who
can come *during the week*. There
is also a children's membership
scheme. Children can join this
scheme if they are between
fifteen and eighteen years old.
Please note that children of less
than fifteen can't come to the
club without an adult and they
can't take sessions on the sun bed
– not that young people usually
want to use a sun bed anyway.
The children's schemes are all
half-price, that is *50 per cent* for
each child or young person in
the scheme. People who live
outside the area can have a
discount of up to 50 per cent, but
this has to be arranged specially

with the general manager. If that is of interest to any of you, let me know and I will fix up an appointment for you. Now, let's go on our tour.

Unit 10

Topic talk

1

a Students' own answer.

b It is perhaps a bit of both. Most individuals can only make small changes within society, which have an impact over time. Some individuals, like scientists and artists, can make huge changes through their work. Society also shapes individuals; otherwise it would be difficult for people to fit in.

c For example, they can help other people who are less able than themselves or less fortunate. They can also aim to make a contribution to society by working hard.

2

b	difficulty	f	outline
c	aspect	h	alternative
d	area	i	attitudes
e	issue		

3

1	f h	3	b c d e
2	g		

4

a proposals
b problem, obstacle, hurdle
c facet
e question
f summary, sketch
g plan
h viewpoints

5

a *topics* replaces *issues*
b *influence* replaces *impact*
c *effect* replaces *impact*
d *theories* replaces *thinking*
e *concerns* replaces *problems*
f *requirement* replaces *necessity*
g *need* replaces *necessity*

6

a international water preservation programme/ research into management of assets

b trade and political partnerships/sharing information and technology

c trade and political partnerships/investing strategically in job creation/ sharing ideas on how to cope with changes/research into management of assets

d flood prevention/research into management of assets/sharing ideas on how to cope with changes

e sharing ideas on how to cope with changes

f research into management of assets/sharing ideas on how to cope with changes/investing strategically in job creation

g trade and political partnerships/investing strategically in job creation/ sharing information and technology/sharing ideas on how to cope with changes

7

Students' own answers.

Listening skills

1

Students' own answers.

2

Students' own answers.

3

Question 2

4

Possible answers

1 Solomon Asch was born in … . The birthplace of Solomon Asch was … .

3 The experiment, which later became so well-known, was called the … .
Asch's famous experiment was known as the … .

4 The people who took part were mostly … .
The subjects of the experiment were for the most part … .

5

1 Poland
2 human behaviour
3 line judgement task
4 actors

Script

Lecturer In this lecture I want to introduce you to the life and work of a famous psychologist, a psychologist who had a big influence on the field of social psychology. Social psychology deals with group behaviour and the individual as a member of a group, and Solomon Asch made a most important contribution. Solomon Asch worked mostly in the USA, but he was born in 1907 in *Poland*, and he came to the US when he was thirteen. He went to an ordinary high school, and as he had an interest in *human behaviour* he decided to study psychology. He was quite disappointed with his first acquaintance with psychology – it seemed to be all about rats and mice and that didn't interest him at all. However, he persevered and eventually became a professor of psychology.

Now, the experiment which made his name is called the *line judgement task*. Participants were asked to compare some simple lines: more precisely, they were given a card with three lines, then were asked to compare another single line and say whether it was longer or shorter than the lines on the card. What a participant didn't know was that in reality, all the other participants were effectively *actors*: that is, they were instructed to give a wrong judgement, and the purpose of the experiment was to see how the single subject would react.

6

The pie-chart in B.

7

A   The pie-chart shows that 68 per cent of people gave the wrong answer, whereas 32 per cent gave the right answer.

C   The pie-chart shows that 32 per cent of people gave the wrong answer, whereas 68 per cent gave the right answer.

8

Possible answers

A   There are three vertical lines, side by side, equal distances apart. The shortest line is on the left, the middle-sized line is in the middle, and the longest line is on the right.

B   The diagram shows three vertical lines of different heights. The tallest is on the left, the shortest is on the right. In the middle is the middle-sized line. They are equal distances apart.

C   This illustration shows three lines of different heights, side by side and equal distances apart. The tallest line is in the middle and the shortest is on the left of it. The middle-sized line is on the right.

9

| 5 | C | 7, 8 | A, E |
| 6 | A | 9, 10 | A, B |

Script

Lecturer   The subject would hear the others saying things about the length of the line which were clearly false. Most subjects answered correctly in spite of the incorrect judgements of the others, but a proportion – 32 per cent – conformed to the majority view, the incorrect view. This proportion was much, much higher than anticipated. Before the experiments they'd thought fifteen per cent or lower might do this. To give you a bit more detail, I have an illustration up here on the board. A group of six or seven people were given a card with three lines on it. There is a short vertical line, on the right of which is a longer line, and on the right of that there is another still longer line. However, it's clear that the longest line is the right-hand one, the second longest the middle one, and the shortest is the one on the left. The participants were given a second card with just one line on it. I should add that in these experiments people became very distressed. They found it very hard to deal with a situation where people were telling them things which were against the evidence of their own eyes. One woman became extremely agitated, running about measuring and looking and checking and shouting in a kind of massive anxiety. Now, what experiments which occurred some time later found was that other factors can influence the result. For example, when there were more so-called participants, there was even more conformity. On the other hand, when people were able to respond in secrecy, by writing the result down for instance, they made fewer incorrect judgements about the lines. Subjects gave various explanations for why they made the decisions they did. Although they weren't put under pressure by the experimenter, many felt that they would somehow spoil the experiment and upset the person running it if they didn't agree, no matter how stupid they felt. More simply, in other cases they said they just wanted to not show themselves in a bad light. Whatever the reason, Asch's experiment has had a long history and …

Speaking skills

1

Text 1:   office, workplace
Text 2:   seaside, beach

2

Students' own answers.

3

a	busy	e	exciting
b	dull	f	friendly
c	deserted	g	peaceful
d	wild	h	colourful

4

a	busy	crowded
b	dull	boring
c	deserted	empty
d	wild	remote
e	exciting	vibrant
f	friendly	welcoming
g	peaceful	quiet
h	colourful	sensuous

5

Students' own answers.

6

Students' own answers.

7

a   Speaker 3: a good atmosphere
b   Speaker 2: it's mine; I can relax there; gets rid of stress
c   Speaker 1: fantastic for walking; an amazing atmosphere

Script

Speaker 1 The place I've decided to talk about is Dartmoor, which is in the south of England. I used to spend a lot of holidays there when I was young. It's a really wild place, fantastic for walking. It's got an amazing atmosphere.

Speaker 2 The place that's really important to me is my garden. It's not very big, but it's mine, and I know I can relax there. Looking after the flowers always gets rid of any stress. And it's colourful too.

Speaker 3 I've chosen to talk about a cafe I go to in town. It's where I go to meet my friends. There's always a good atmosphere, and it's nice to just sit and watch other people walking past.

8

Speaker 1: The place I've decided to talk about is …
Speaker 2: The place that's really important to me is …
Speaker 3: I've chosen to talk about a … I go to.

9

Students' own answers.

10

Possible answers

1 a, d
2 b, d, e, f, g
3 a, c

11

Students' own answers.

12

a /d/   d /t/
b /t/   e /Id/
c /t/

Script

I tried a parachuting course last year.
I liked it a lot.
I almost panicked in the plane.
But I jumped.
I landed very softly – thank goodness.

13

1 started /Id/
2 climbed /d/
3 picnicked /t/
4 watched /t/
5 camped /t/
6 collected /Id/
7 started /Id/
8 arrived /d/
9 enjoyed /d/

Exam listening

Questions 21–24

21 A   23 B
22 C   24 A

Script

Mike Well, Fiona, we certainly have a lot of work to do this weekend. I wish now I hadn't spent so much time on my other assignment.

Fiona Don't say that! You did really well: 80 per cent.

Mike Yes, but this is different. It's not hard really, it's just all a bit of a rush. We had loads of time to get the other one right, but this one is all a bit pressured. That's what makes me anxious, despite the preparation we've done.

Fiona You shouldn't worry. What could go wrong? Look, let's look through what we can do to make sure it's OK.

Mike Well, the main difficulty that's bothering me is about defining the terms of reference. It's supposed to be about approaches to social welfare, right.

Fiona Yes, but we're not expected to give a survey of what that means. That's not the point. We're supposed to be comparing the way welfare is approached in collectivist societies and what you might call capitalist societies.

Mike So we can concentrate on just that contrast.

Fiona Yes.

Mike The other thing that bothers me is that I'm not really committed to either view.

Fiona Well, I have strong opinions of my own, but that's not supposed to colour my judgement.

Mike How do you mean?

Fiona Well, what you write for this is supposed to be unbiased. It specifically says that you shouldn't give a personal view.

Mike But Professor Green has a personal view.

Fiona Yes, but that doesn't mean that we have to agree with him, and I don't think we'll do any better if we do.

Mike And how long does it have to be?

Fiona The maximum is 4,000 words.

Mike What?

Fiona But that's the maximum. We'll probably end up with about three, but at least 2,000 is the minimum. Shouldn't be a problem.

Mike Mm. OK.

Questions 25 and 26

25 the Welfare State
26 Tuesday(s)

Questions 27–30

27 Welfare Economics
28 Mike Green
29 Growing old
30 2005

Script

Mike Now where can we get some information on all this?

Fiona Well, we could ask Olive over there. Olive, you did this assignment last year, didn't you?

Olive Not this one exactly, but something similar. The most important thing is to get Professor Green's lectures on *The Welfare State*.

Mike Is he good?

Olive Oh, very good. Didn't you know he was lecturing?

Fiona No, no idea.

Olive Well, he is. He's at the Becket Building on *Tuesdays*. I think he's starting this week, so you'll be able to get the series of six. He deals with the underlying philosophy as well as the economics of it all. It's at 10 a.m. – I'd go myself except that I have too much to do.

Mike And what about reading? I've got the reading list here. As usual, it has far more titles and references than we can possibly read in the time.

Fiona I haven't even got a reading list. Where did you get that from, Mike?

Mike I got it at the welcome lecture.

Fiona Oh. I wish I'd gone to that now.

Olive What you need above all is his own book, called *Welfare Economics*. All the department know it and follow his approach.

Mike Oh, right, good idea. Perhaps we don't need to go to the lecture if we have his book?

Olive No, I really do advise you to go to his lectures as well.

Fiona Well, what was the full title of his book?

Olive If I remember rightly, it's called, simply *Welfare Economics*, by *Mike Green*.

Mike I've got it. *Welfare Economics*, Glenfield University Press, 2006.

Fiona Great. Let me just write that down.

Mike Anything else you recommend?

Olive There's Edward Jones's book, erm, *Growing Old in Britain*. That's essential reading but you have to be careful, because it's a popular book by a journalist.

Fiona Well, if it's popular, maybe we'll like it. Who publishes that?

Mike That's published by Rutland University Press in *2005*.

Fiona Well, that's very useful. I think it's Professor Green for us next.

Mike Right.